Go Your Own Least Cost Path

Spatial technology and archaeological interpretation

Proceedings of the GIS session at EAA 2009, Riva del Garda

Edited by

P. Verhagen
A. G. Posluschny
A. Danielisová

BAR International Series 2284
2011

Published in 2016 by
BAR Publishing, Oxford

BAR International Series 2284

Go Your Own Least Cost Path

ISBN 978 1 4073 0861 6

BAR Publishing is the trading name of British Archaeological Reports (Oxford) Ltd.
British Archaeological Reports was first incorporated in 1974 to publish the BAR
Series, International and British. In 1992 Hadrian Books Ltd became part of the BAR
group. This volume was originally published by Archaeopress in conjunction with
British Archaeological Reports (Oxford) Ltd / Hadrian Books Ltd, the Series principal
publisher, in 2011. This present volume is published by BAR Publishing, 2016.

Printed in England

BAR
PUBLISHING

BAR titles are available from:

BAR Publishing
122 Banbury Rd, Oxford, OX2 7BP, UK
EMAIL   info@barpublishing.com
PHONE   +44 (0)1865 310431
FAX   +44 (0)1865 316916
www.barpublishing.com

Content

Preface

In September 2009, the European Association of Archaeologists held its 15th Annual Meeting in Riva del Garda, Italy. At this conference, we organized a session with the title 'Go your own least cost path – Spatial technology and archaeological interpretation'. The original session proposal reads as follows:

Geographical Information Systems (GIS) have gradually become an indispensible tool for archaeologists. A number of powerful software tools, some developed by archaeologists themselves, are now used for spatial research questions like settlement history, territorial analyses, land use development, landscape perception and many more. The main focus so far in various GIS sessions at archaeological conferences has been on the methods and theories of GIS, on technical issues, and the development and use of new techniques and algorithms. Furthermore, many published GIS-applications do not move very far beyond the descriptive stage.

The aim of this session is to take a look at what results GIS delivers for archaeological interpretation and how the use of spatial technologies influences research design. We therefore encourage participants to present papers that focus on the role and perception of GIS in their research. Case studies are welcomed that show examples of GIS-based landscape or intra-site research. Questions that could be addressed are:

- *What is the added value of GIS to archaeological interpretation, and what are the limitations?*
- *Can GIS be used successfully as a central research framework that allows researchers to combine their data in one environment and achieve a better interaction and dialogue between disciplines?*
- *How do we find the right methods and tools to deal with our data?*
- *How do we deal with the debate between the scientistic and interpretative schools of archaeology?*
- *How do we deal with the GIS based interpretations within our own scientific environments (academic debate, our countries etc.)*
- *Do the GIS based interpretations change the embedded perceptions of the past?*

In total we received 18 paper proposals, of which 11 were eventually presented at the conference in a lively and well attended session; 7 more papers were presented as posters. From the start, it was our intention to publish as many of the papers and posters as possible in a proceedings volume. In this volume you will find the 7 papers that were eventually written on the basis of the original presentations. The other authors declined to contribute, mostly because of time constraints, or because they felt the research presented was not ready for publication yet. While we respect the personal motivations for this, we also suspect that this may be a consequence of the current research climate in Europe, where scientific status is becoming more and more dependent on the number of publications in A-rated journals. Conference proceedings, even when they are peer-reviewed, are the most obvious victims of this development. We are therefore especially thankful to the authors who did take the effort to write a paper for this volume.

While obviously not covering the whole range of subjects that were addressed during the session, we feel that the papers collected in this volume still give an adequate overview of the kind of questions that archaeologists use GIS for nowadays. It is not our intention to produce a state-of-the-art of current developments in archaeological GIS here, since two reviews have recently appeared that do just that (Wagtendonk et al. 2009; McCoy and Ladefoged 2009). However, within the context of this volume we want to draw the reader's attention to a few important aspects of current GIS use in archaeology. The first of these is the breadth of archaeological GIS applications nowadays. We have now finally arrived at the stage where GIS is no longer just used at the (micro-)regional level, but also at the intra-site level. We also witness an increasing level of data integration in archaeological GIS applications.

It is also clear that spatial modelling is becoming more and more accepted as a way of setting up archaeological hypotheses and testing them. The whole debate on GIS within the context of processual versus post-processual archaeology and the criticism on environmental determinism (e.g. Gaffney and van Leusen 1995; Wheatley 2004) is becoming outdated, now that spatial models more and more try to include aspects of human decision making and agency explicitly, instead of just relying on descriptive data of the natural environment and archaeological site records. In our view, this is an important step forward compared to the way GIS was used until the early 2000s, and cannot be attributed to the technological advancement of the software – which in fact has only been marginal over the past 10 years. It is a clear sign of the maturing of our discipline when it comes to applying GIS, and it constitutes a compliment to the many practitioners who have experimented with spatial modelling over the past 20 years.

However, we have to be aware that successful application of GIS-techniques still depends on skilled practitioners. We have long left the age where archaeologists would be found completely helpless in the presence of GIS without the aid of a computer 'nerd'. Current software is much more user-friendly (and cheaper); however, the effective use of GIS still requires the execution of time-consuming operations ranging from digitizing and database management to programming, that need the appropriate professional skills to be executed effectively and efficiently. In that sense, GIS is no longer different to other specializations found in archaeology, and eventually we may see the emergence of a sub-discipline of 'spatial archaeology', whose practitioners will work in teams with other specialists. Since geographical data are so central to almost all archaeological research, it can be expected that these 'spatial archaeologists' will play a pivotal role in many research projects.

The papers in this volume have been organized in a loose thematic order, moving from heritage management to regional studies to intra-site research. The themes addressed in each paper are actually quite different, and forms another proof of the breadth of GIS applications today.

In chapter 1, Jeffrey Altschul and colleagues report on a predictive modelling project in Senegal. They have chosen a new direction in predictive modelling working in a region with little reliable archaeological evidence. This absence of evidence made them think along very different lines than is usual in predictive modelling, and to investigate the potential of ethnographical theory and agent-based models to infer cultural behaviours that might have led to the differential deposition of archaeological remains.

In chapter 2, Wivianne Bondesson and colleagues present a report on a typical cultural heritage management application in Sweden, where planners and policy makers depend on multi-disciplinary data to evaluate the cultural values in a region, and to define management goals for these values. GIS is indispensable for this as a means to visualize the value of the cultural landscape, and to start a dialogue not only between practitioners of different scientific disciplines, but also between scientist, planners, politicians and the general public.

In chapter 3, Andrey Mazurkevich and Ekaterina Dolbunova describe the use of GIS in a regional study of the Early and Middle Neolithic settlement system in NW Russia. Despite the fact that their GIS analyses only use standard tools available in ArcGIS, their study shows that even with relatively simple techniques a number of new conclusions can be drawn about the development of Early and Middle Neolithic settlement in the area.

In chapter 4, Alžběta Danielisová and Petr Pokorný describe their attempts to combine palaeo-ecological and archaeological data in GIS to reconstruct the past cultural landscape around the Vladař hillfort in the Czech Republic. The problems associated with spatializing the punctual pollen records into land use maps for different time slices are considerable, but their paper opens up a whole new range of possibilities for past landscape reconstruction.

In chapter 5, Hèctor Orengo and Carme Miró report how they combined least cost route modelling and the analysis of historical cartographic sources to establish if the aqueducts of Barcelona, known from medieval sources, are of Roman origin.

In chapter 6, Petr Květina and Markéta Končelová describe how GIS is used to analyse the formation processes of pit fills in the Bylany site in the Czech Republic. While GIS modelling is not central to the argument of natural versus intentional fill, 3-dimensional representations and statistical analysis of artifact concentrations in the pits are essential to support the argument that these pit fillings were mainly the result of intentional human activity.

And lastly, in chapter 7 Richard Thér and Jan Prostředník use intra-site spatial analysis to support their hypothesis that the large amount of Late Bronze Age overfired pottery found in Eastern Bohemia is related to settlement fires rather then to firing technology.

It is hoped that the papers in this volume may serve as inspiration to archaeologists seeking to apply spatial analysis in their research. By focusing on the archaeological implications, rather than the technical and methodological issues involved, we think that it will be easier for non-GIS-experts to understand the potential and limitations of spatial analysis. Hopefully, it will encourage them to consider the technology not just as a means to describe and visualize geographical data, but also as a useful tool to address interpretive archaeological questions and develop new hypotheses.

The editors

Philip Verhagen   –   Axel G. Posluschny   –   Alžběta Danielisová

References Cited

GAFFNEY, V. – VAN LEUSEN, P. M. 1995: Postscript—GIS, environmental determinism and archaeology: a parallel text. In: Lock, G. – Stančič, Z. (eds.): *Archaeology and Geographical Information Systems: A European Perspective*, London, 367–382.

McCOY, M.D. – LADEFOGED, T.N. 2009: New Developments in the Use of Spatial Technology in Archaeology. *Journal of Archaeological Research* 17, 26 –295.

WAGTENDONK, A. – VERHAGEN, P. – SOETENS, S. – JENESON, K. – DE KLEIJN, M. 2009: Past in Place: The Role of Geo-ICT in Present-day Archaeology. In: Scholten, H. J. – van de Velde, R. – van Manen, N. (eds.), *Geospatial Technology and the Role of Location in Science*, Dordrecht (GeoJournal Library 96), 59–86.

WHEATLEY, D. 2004: Making Space for an Archaeology of Place. *Internet Archaeology* 15, http://intarch.ac.uk/journal/issue15/wheatley_index.html.

P. Verhagen, A. G. Posluschny, A. Danielisová (eds.)
Proceedings EAA 2009: Go Your Own Least Cost Path, Riva del Garda

Incorporating GIS Methodological Approaches in Heritage Management Projects

Jeffrey H. Altschul, Richard Ciolek-Torrello, Michael Heilen, William Hayden, Jeffrey A. Homburg,
Gerry Wait, Ibrahima Thiaw

Abstract

There has been a long-standing debate in academic archaeology on how to study the surface archaeological record.
The debate has centered around whether to interpret the
record as consisting of discrete sites and isolates or as
continuous distributions of artifacts, features, and deposits. Historic preservation laws, however, focus on discrete
sites as the properties that need to be discovered, recorded,
and evaluated. As more research is done within a heritage
management framework, the outcome has been to focus on
the site as the unit of analysis almost to the exclusion of
the study of spatial behaviors that transcend discrete sites.
To achieve the objectives of heritage preservation and
to examine spatial human behavior that is unconstrained
by the site concept, new methodologies are needed. As a
move in this direction we use GIS to create hypothetical
archaeological landscapes based on assumptions of human
behavior that can be tested and refined with survey and
excavation data. In this process we collect detailed surface
data that GIS algorithms use to define discrete sites and,
at the same time, to analyze continuous distributions of
cultural materials. We illustrate this approach with a several examples from North America and West Africa using
different field methodologies.

Introduction

In heritage management, archaeologists are often asked to
answer three basic questions: How many sites are in a project area? Where are these sites located? And, which sites
are important enough to be investigated more thoroughly?
Answering these questions requires us to use existing information on culture and the environment to design surveys, incorporate new data as they are obtained from the
field to assess survey adequacy, and to infer cultural behaviors from settlement and resource locations. GIS technology provides a single platform from which these three
endeavors can be performed in an efficient, objective, and
replicable manner. Much of what follows has been placed
under the rubric of predictive modeling. As we demonstrate, however, the term now encompasses a much wider
array of models and modeling techniques than in the past.
One of the uses of predictive modeling is to guide invento-
ry effort. The basic approach is to use archaeological data
collected from a part (i.e., sample) of a specified region
(the sample universe) to create an environmental signature
of where sites tend to be located and generalize it to the rest
of the sample universe. Using multiple regression or logistic regression, an equation can be created by which independent environmental variables are statistically related to
predict the likelihood that a particular area will contain an

archaeological site (Rose/Altschul 1988). The advantage
of using environmental variables is that the variable states
of interest can be continually mapped across the surface of
the sample universe. For interval scale data, such as elevation, a unique score can be assigned to any particular parcel. For categorical variables, like landforms, the sample
universe can be divided into a series of polygons, each representing a particular landform, and each parcel within the
polygon receiving the same "landform" score. Predictive
statements tend to become more accurate as archaeological surveys cover more area and become more representative of the range of scores for each environmental variable
used to predict site location. In essence, confidence in a
model's predictions increases as the sample fraction of the
entire universe increases and more diverse environmental
settings are surveyed.

Regression models as well as simpler intersection, or correlative, models became extremely popular with the ad-
vent of GIS technology. GIS software provided the means
for dividing areas into small cells that could adequately
capture environmental variation affecting human behavior
as well as making the enormous number of calculations
required by multivariate statistical techniques quickly
and easily. Generally, the main output of GIS software is
graphic in nature; sensitivity maps which show the likelihood that a particular parcel contains an archaeological
site have become standard fare in archaeological management.

Regression and correlative models are based on the assumption that human behavior is patterned. Decisions
about where to establish settlements or conduct activities
are conditioned by a set of cultural "rules," such as how
close to be to specific resources, how best to shield one-
self from enemies, and so on. Archaeologists are generally
not privy to these rules. If these decisions are patterned,
however, the resulting behaviors will yield a particular distribution of archaeological sites and materials. Archaeologists, then, can infer the basis of these settlement decisions
by associating site locations with their environmental settings. This logic is the basis for many types of archaeological investigations, ranging from site catchment analysis of
single site locations to regional settlement pattern analysis.

Like site catchment or regional analyses, most predictive
modeling begins with the assumption that human behavior
is patterned according to environmental variables. Predictive modeling differs from other analytical approaches to
studying human spatial behavior by stopping short of developing or requiring a framework for explaining observed
patterns. Humans may adapt to their environment in complex ways, but the result is that archaeological sites tend to

be associated with particular environmental settings. Even if we do not understand the underlying adaptation, we can still predict site location. By the same token, finding associations between environmental characteristics and site location can lead to unexpected insights regarding the factors influencing settlement decisions. Altschul and his colleagues (ALTSCHUL ET AL. 2005, 49) present the logic of using environmental variables to predict human use of a landscape in southeast New Mexico as follows:

- The environmental variables used in predictive models are best viewed as proxy variables.
- Humans use a complicated "calculus" in assessing potential locations in which to live, obtain and process resources, and commune with their gods.
- People do not generally measure the slope of the land where they place their houses or measure the exact distance to water, but they do choose land that is flat and near water.
- The indigenous people of Loco Hills probably did not know, much less care, at what elevation they placed their camps, but they certainly knew where the stands of black grama and tobosa grasses occurred.
- Elevation, though not part of the prehistoric "calculus," is strongly correlated with the vegetative communities of southeast New Mexico and thus can be used as a predictor of site location.

For some planning and management purposes, just knowing where sites are located, or are likely to be located, is enough. For example, the locations of well pads used to explore for oil and gas can be moved so as to avoid sites. Hence, by adopting a "flag and avoid" strategy, archaeologists working with oil and gas producers do not need to know anything about a site other than its boundaries. Similarly, during the initial stages of planning a road, it is probably sufficient to know the relative likelihood that each possible alignment will cross archaeological sites as opposed to the exact number and nature of the potentially affected sites.

In many cases, however, we need to know more. Decisions about which archaeological sites to protect, which ones to disturb, which sites need to be investigated, and how much of each site needs to be excavated, require that we distinguish between sites on the basis of their scientific importance. To accomplish this, we need to develop and test hypotheses about why sites are located where they are, which means we need to understand the adaptation underlying settlement decisions.

In areas with long archaeological traditions, human adaptations have generally been explored with some rigor so that the patterns expressed in predictive models can be readily incorporated into theoretical models of settlement and subsistence. Combining empirically based projections of settlement trends with theoretical notions about subsistence practices often leads to the selection of samples of sites to excavate that have a strong potential to advance

our understanding of the past. Such is not the case, however, in regions that have been largely ignored by archaeologists. In these situations, we must use the initial survey data to tease out broad trends in settlement and to hypothesize about the kinds of land-use behaviors that could have resulted in the observed pattern. These dual requirements are even more critical for development projects for which the time between survey and excavation is compressed, so that information needs to be developed quickly about which sites or site components are important enough to warrant further investigation and/or protection. Instead of relying less on models, these situations cry out for a greater reliance on tools that not only help archaeologists interpret survey results but also help communicate to regulators and other stakeholders what we think is important about the past and how many sites, and how much of each site, we need to excavate, so that appropriate heritage decisions can be made.

Cultural heritage is not simply about saving vestiges of the past; it is also about ensuring that traditions and traditional ways of life are preserved and enhanced in the face of modern development. Often, decisions about social impacts of development are made without properly taking into account a region's culture history or traditional socioeconomic adaptation. The result is that economic development is commonly followed by disruption of traditional social institutions. The lives of many of the individuals that the "aid" is designed to improve are actually made worse. Archaeologists are in a unique position to address this problem. By studying how humans adapt to a particular environment over long periods and how changes in these adaptations affect social, economic, and political institutions, archaeologists can provide insights into how a particular culture might react to proposed changes.

GIS technology has led to the development of a powerful tool, agent-based modeling, which provides a framework for testing different theories of adaptation. Unlike regression or correlative predictive models in which patterns of settlement are inductively derived from generalizing patterns from the known (i.e., surveyed areas in the sample universe) to the unknown (i.e., non surveyed areas in the sample universe), agent-based modeling begins with a linked set of logical statements about how human actors (either individuals or groups) behave in a particular landscape. The model unfolds as actors respond to environmental events (i.e., drought, fish runs, etc.) and the consequence of their own actions (e.g., overgrazing, surplus harvest for trade, etc.). By running each adaptive scenario numerous times, and then again under slightly different rules or parameters, the range in settlement variation for each adaptation can be documented.

Comparing the results of correlative predictive models of archaeological site location and agent-based models of human adaptation can lead to interesting insights. In theory, the two should be linked because human land-use behavior will be related to the distribution of archaeological materials. Although postdepositional processes can account for

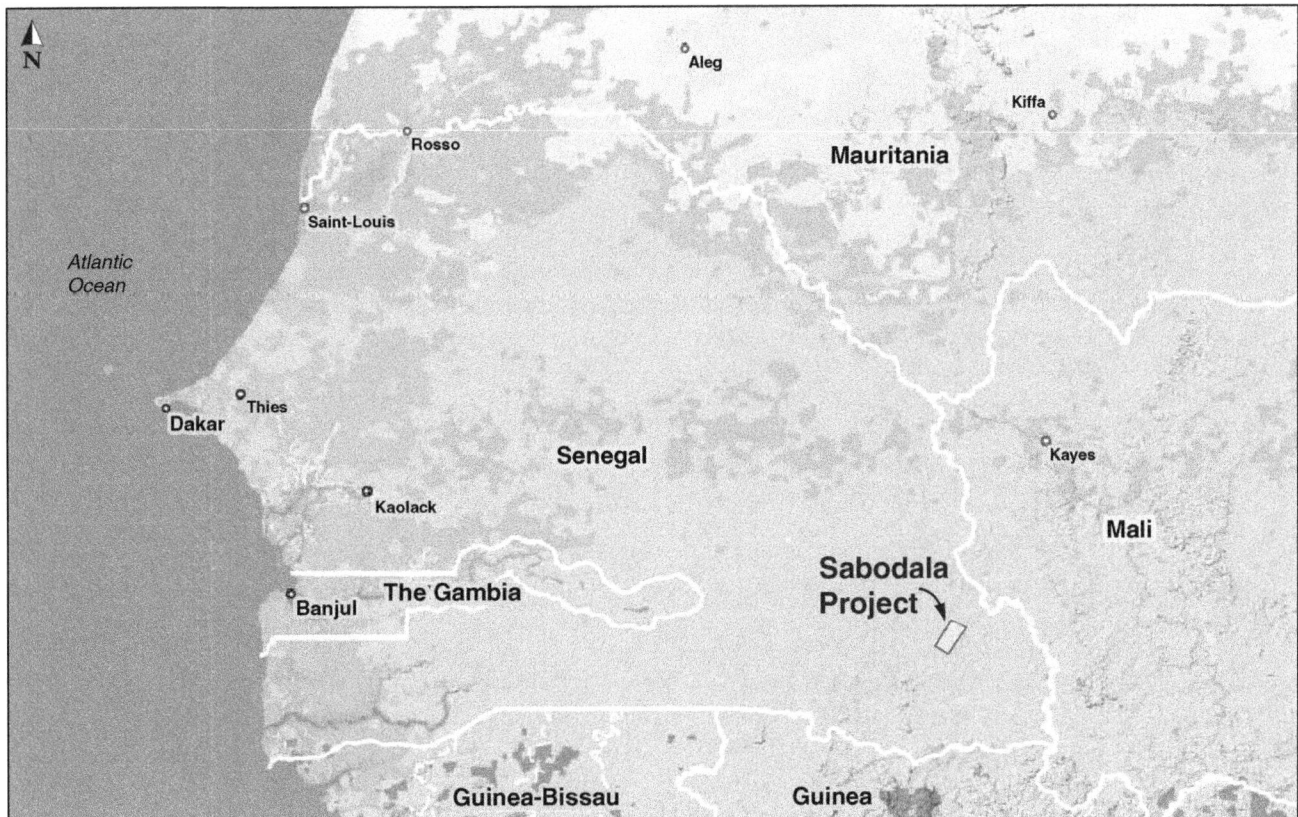

Figure 1. The Sabodala Project Area.

some of the discrepancies between the results from the two types of models, more fundamental differences – such as the same environmental zone being considered favorable for settlement by inductively based models and unfavorable by the deductive agent-based models – probably signifies that one or more of the proxy variables in the correlative models is not related to human behavior and/or that one or more of the adaptive "rules" in the agent-based models is wrong. Regardless, these discrepancies point to fruitful lines of future research.

As our ability to explain the connections between the two modeling approaches increases, we will be in a better position to predict how future development will impact a particular society. Instead of being viewed as interesting, but not terribly useful, archaeology can become an important element in discussions of socioeconomic development. Ultimately, understanding the past will assist in shaping a positive future.

In this paper, we present our approach to one such case of economic development from the Sabodala region of east Senegal. We begin with a brief discussion of the area, its archaeology, environment, and culture. We then present the results of correlative predictive models of surface sites and a geomorphic predictive model of buried sites. Next, we discuss our approach to agent-based modeling for the study of long-term human adaptation to the region. We close with a statement about modeling in development contexts.

Sabodala

Our study area is a 240 km² region at the upper reaches of the Senegal River and Gambia River drainages *(figure 1)*. The Senegal and Gambia Rivers both rise in the highlands of Guinea and flow northwest to the Atlantic Ocean. The Senegal River flows along the eastern and northern borders of Senegal, dividing it from Mali and Mauritania. The Gambia River flows through southern Senegal, with its lowest reach contained within the tiny country of The Gambia. Ephemeral streams flow north from the project area merging with the Falemme River, a major tributary of the Senegal River, about 40 km to the northeast on the Senegal-Mali border. Similar streams flow into the Senegal plains to the west and south before being captured by the Gambia River about 100 km to the southwest of the project area. Several mining concessions have been defined, and we are engaged in completing the cultural heritage component of the economic and social impact assessment of one of those concessions. In 2009, we conducted the first phase of ethnographic research, compiled historic maps and documents, and created the initial predictive models of archaeological site location. Archaeological monitoring of exploration activities began in 2010; archaeological and ethnographic field surveys are scheduled for later this year.

The Sabodala region is hilly and volcanic and receives on average a little more than a meter of rain per year, mostly in the wet season from June until September. Rainfall, however, is extremely variable, and the well-drained volcanic and sedimentary rock regime ensures that outside of the rainy season surface water is scarce. Paleoclimatic evidence suggests that except for relatively brief periods, the region has been hot and dry for most of the Holocene (THIAW 1999). This is particularly true for the last 500 years. It is not the aridity, however, that is of most concern to human settlement. More important are the large interannual fluctuations in climate and the periodic long intervals of drought conditions.

No systematic archaeological work has been performed in the general area. In the early twentieth century, fascination with Acheulean hand axes and Neolithic stone axes fueled interest in the archaeology of eastern Senegal. LAFORGUE (1923, 1925) mentions the Sabodala region in an early review of the prehistory of the Sahara and West Africa. Professional archaeological research in Senegal, however, only took root after the foundation of IFAN (Institut Français d'Afrique Noire, or French Institute for Black Africa) in 1936. IFAN sponsored inventories throughout West Africa that resulted in a number of syntheses of the massive database (GUITAT 1970; MAUNY 1961; RAVISÉ 1970). Sites in eastern Senegal were reported, although none were recorded in the project area or its immediate surroundings. The closest systematic work consisted of a 50-km survey and limited testing at three sites performed by THIAW (1999) as part of his dissertation on the lower Falemme River, located more than 100 km to the north. Ceramic and other artifact classifications applied to Sabodala derive from the Middle Senegal Valley Project of 1990–1992, which focused on large sites on the Senegal River, located more than 200 km to the north (MCINTOSH ET AL. 1992). Both of these studies focused on alluvial settings of major drainages, not upland areas, and the suitability of generalizing existing results to the upper Senegal and upper Gambia drainages has not been demonstrated.

Today, agriculture and pastoralism are the main subsistence activities in the region, with artisanal gold mining another major economic activity. Agriculture is largely dependent on rainfall. Unlike the better studied areas of the Senegal River and its major tributaries, such as the Falemme, where recession agriculture predominates, Sabodala has no perennial streams, and the floodplains that exist are extremely narrow. Soils are deepest and best suited for agriculture in constrained alluvial settings; however, soil development also has occurred on plateau-like areas on the tops of hills. Slash and burn is the most common technique to clear farmland; it is also used to hunt game and to stimulate fresh grass and clear out thorny vegetation for cattle and goats.

Although today pastoralism is very important, it is unlikely that such was the case in the more distant past. The climate in West Africa was sufficiently wet that the tse tse fly would have impeded the development of pastoralism until about 500 years ago.

Artisanal gold mining has been practiced in the hills of Senegal since at least the rise of Islam in West Africa (THI-AW 1999). For the most part, gold mining was an adjunct to other subsistence activities. The gold mine trade has historically been controlled by North African traders who maintained the trade routes through the Sahara and local brokers and merchants known as Juula, who were generally Soninke or Malinke people. This practice continues today, with much of the gold being bought by traders based in the adjoining country of Mali. Gold mining is practiced through an intricate social organization in which the mining is completed by male task groups that sell the excavated "dirt" to family-based groups, who in turn sluice and process the gold.

The Sabodala region is occupied presently by a variety of ethnic and linguistic groups. Communities of two linguistic groups – Malinke and Peul – dominate the region and exert the greatest influence on social and political institutions. Malinke and Peul societies are typically stratified and are subdivided into three classes: nobles, "castes," and slaves. Although these classes are still recognized, they have been subverted and reshuffled in complex ways. For example, slavery is outlawed in Senegal; yet, because status is ascribed, the term "slave" is still used to refer to descendants, and master/slave relations have been largely transformed into relations of clientage (THIAW 1998).

The ethnographic evidence we collected indicates that the communities in the Sabodala region are likely uprooted and have emigrated from neighboring regions of Senegal, Mali, and Guinea. Lands suitable for agriculture are quite restricted and are controlled by the elites who are predominantly of the Cissoko lineage. The Cissoko control most of the chieftaincies in the local villages of the region. The agricultural potential of other lands is poor, although they are plentiful; lands poorly suited to agriculture are left to the lower classes. Land is inherited within the lineage, which means it is collective in theory; but in practice, members of the lower classes and junior members of elite classes do not have access to quality land. The result is high mobility among these people, who are constantly in search of better land. Much of the tension both within communities and within elite families is related to access to land.

Each village considers the lands within 8–10 km as "theirs" with regard to agriculture and use rights for lands up to 50 km from the village for such activities as herding and hunting. Villages tend to be located adjacent to or near agricultural land and in locations where potable water is near the surface and available year-round. Villages are spaced relatively far apart, separated by vast tracts of land of marginal quality for agriculture. In an absolute sense, therefore, land is never in short supply. Movement is not greatly restricted, and the sociogeographic history of the region is of social groups continually fragmenting and starting new communities. The current population generally claims origin in Mali (either from Tomara, Marena, or Maraka), Guinea (primarily from Fuuta and Djallon), and Senegal (from Bundu and the Middle Senegal valley). It is likely that these immigrants made it to the Sabodala

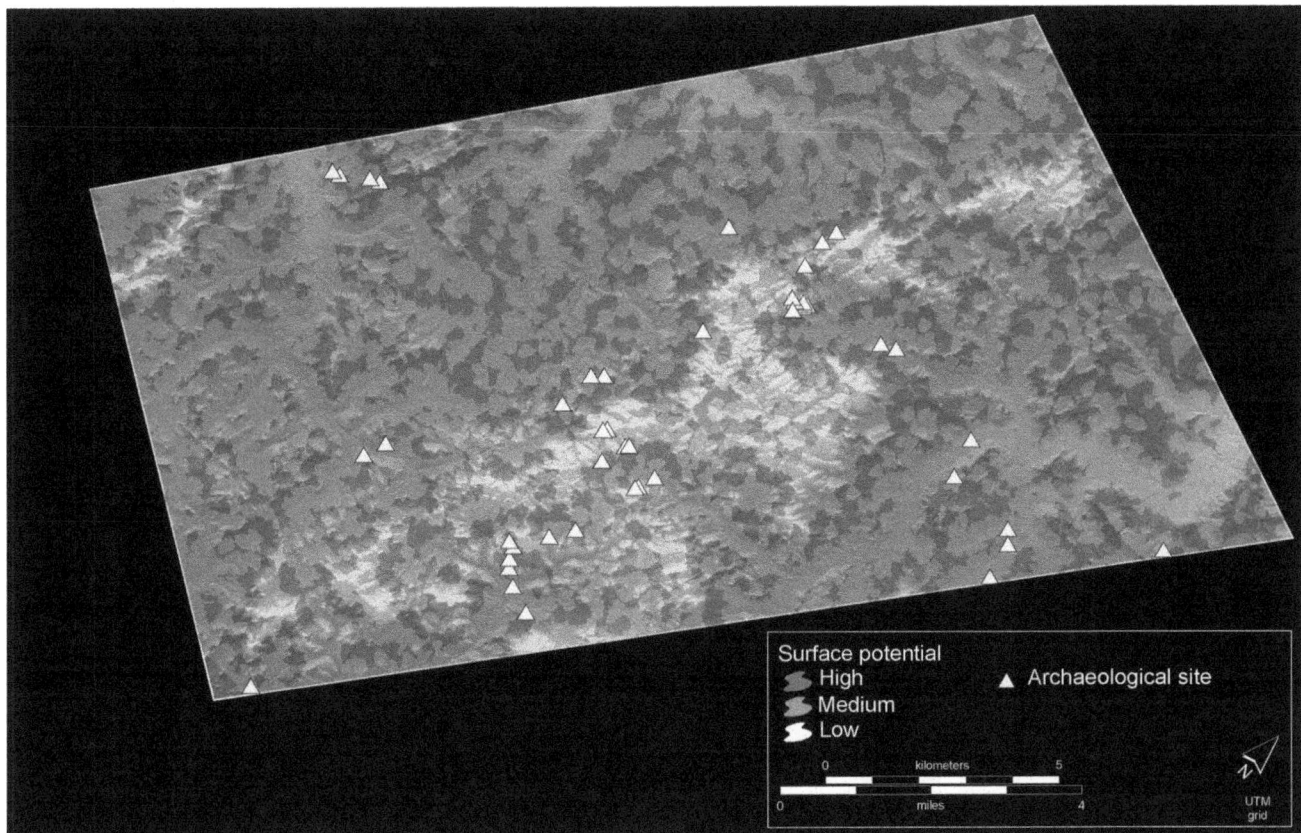

Figure 2. Predictive model of surface archaeological sites, showing locations of known archaeological sites.

area no earlier than the eighteenth or nineteenth centuries, where they established the villages of Mamakono, Sekhoto, and NioMadina. These villages in turn grew and fragmented into the 10 current villages in the nineteenth and twentieth centuries. Whether these groups would have continued to grow and fragment or whether population movement would have continued on further west is unknown. The development of industrial gold mining along with other infrastructure developments, such as irrigation in the Senegal River Valley (PARK 1993), have altered the traditional economic base in fundamental ways.

Correlative Models

The ethnographic survey was designed primarily to identify sacred and traditional places of importance to local residents. In the course of our fieldwork, we identified archaeological sites found along the way. This initial effort resulted in recording 50 traditional sites and identifying 49 archaeological sites. The archaeological sites discovered range from Neolithic villages with associated field houses and activity areas to upper Paleolithic artifact scatters (ca. 40,000–10,000 years ago). Although the survey was cursory and opportunistic, it certainly demonstrated the archaeological and cultural richness of the area.

Our next task is to design a sample that adequately assesses the nature of the archaeological record: the number and types of sites and the time periods represented. In de-

velopment projects, it is not uncommon for only the direct impact zones to be surveyed. Without a regional context in which to place the sample of sites, however, the results of even very intense investigations are highly restricted. In these cases, we select some arbitrary sampling fraction of nonimpact areas for survey, such as 5, 10, 20, or 50 percent, in addition to the impact zones. Often, this strategy leaves archaeologists and nonarchaeologists alike wondering if the survey captured enough archaeological and environmental variation to characterize the archaeological record sufficiently to make sound decisions about heritage. ALTSCHUL ET AL. (2005) have demonstrated that statistical models can be powerful tools in assessing survey results. As more survey is completed, new models can be calculated and compared statistically and visually with previous ones. Particularly for nonarchaeologists, visual comparisons showing site sensitivity zones converging in size and shape as more data are added can be very powerful in decisions about when basic settlement trends are reliably established. By having the GIS model parameters already established at the outset of fieldwork, we can add survey results on an iterative basis and make decisions of survey sufficiency without recourse to a fixed, arbitrary sample fraction. For example, regulators, project sponsors, and archaeologists might agree prior to the survey that high-sensitivity zones should contain 85 percent of the sites in less than a third of the sample universe. The model can be recalculated periodically and the survey continued until the desired model parameters are met.

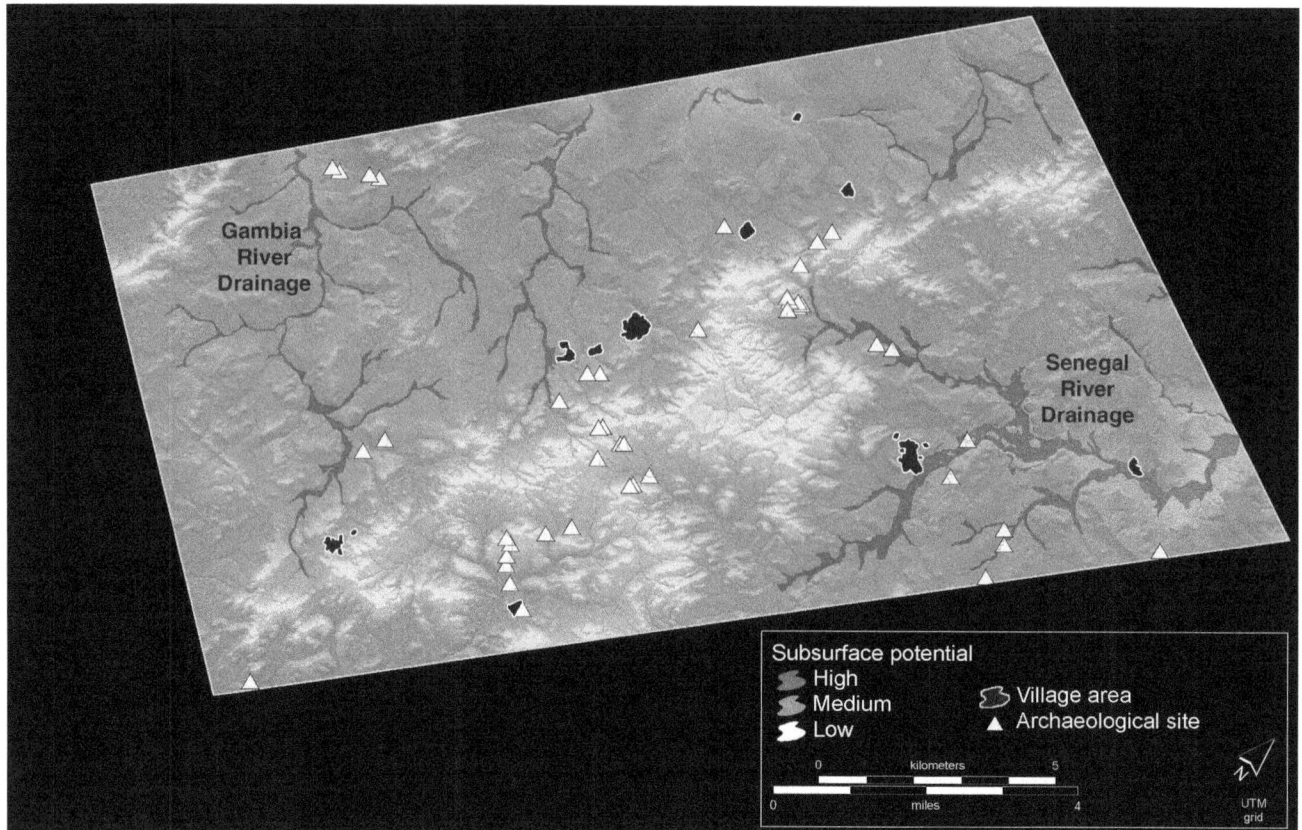

Figure 3. Predictive model of buried archaeological sites, showing locations of known archaeological sites and modern villages.

To create a model of surface archaeological locations, we first determined which environmental variables were associated with known site locations. The sample universe was divided into a large number of small grid cells of equal size and shape that serve as the unit of analysis. We compared the characteristics of five variables – aspect, elevation, flow length (a proxy for runoff accumulation), soil type, and slope – in cells containing archaeological sites with those for the project area as a whole to develop the initial model. It is important to note that we were not able to correlate nonsite locations with environmental variables, as is generally the case with predictive modeling, because we have not systematically surveyed for sites. Thus, we only know where the 49 sites were found, not where archaeological sites have not been found. Consequently, we could not use logistic regression or similar techniques, which distinguish "site" and "nonsite" cells based on their probabilities of belonging to the respective classes. Instead we created a model based on a supervised classification using the IDRISI software package. Using the five environmental variables, we created three categories and ranked them according to the proportion of sites contained in each category to the proportion of cells of the category and to the total number of cells in the sample universe. We then cross-checked the result by computing a Principal Components Analysis (PCA) on the selected variables and performing a supervised classification of the PCA results; the results of the two techniques were very similar.

We found that one of the categories is positively correlated with site locations; we termed this category the high-sensitivity zone. Statistically, high-sensitivity cells were distinguished from cells in the other two categories primarily because they had short flow lengths (180 m average), were facing south, and were lying on greater slopes. High-sensitivity lands accounted for about a third of the project area but nearly half the sites. A second category, termed the low-sensitivity zone, covered nearly 13 percent of the project area, but contained only two sites. Cells of this category were distinguished from the others because they had long flow lengths (850 m average), were facing north, and were on relatively flatter land. The vast area in the middle, called the moderate-sensitivity zone, accounted for just over half the project area and about 46 percent of all site locations.

Figure 2 presents the surface model. Low-sensitivity zones are concentrated in the hills of Sabodala, whereas the high-sensitivity zones cover hill slopes and knolls overlooking watercourses. The vast unknown is pretty much everywhere in between. Because the model is fitted to the data, it is best viewed as a reflection of where we have looked and not necessarily where sites are located. Sites have mostly been found along sections of roads that cross the floodplain and below the hills. We have found a surprising number of sites in these areas, which are properly marked as high sensitivity. The relative sensitivity of the other two zones is very much in doubt. For example, the model classifies most alluvial settings in the moderate-sensitivity zone. Yet, these are precisely where many activities, such as those involving gold mining sluices, agricultural plots, corrals for goats and cattle, soccer fields, and sacred trees, are concentrated. These areas flood periodically, and there is little surface evidence of activities known to be performed there. Beneath the surface, however, may be a different story. Storage features, middens, and other, more-permanent features, such as stone rubble mounds that mark graves, should withstand the scouring of floods and the colluvial deposits washed in from the adjacent hill slopes. Even during the ethnographic survey, when we were not looking very hard, we found one buried site in an alluvial setting.

Detecting buried deposits requires subsurface probing, which is expensive and time consuming. To guide this process, we created a preliminary model of buried site probability for the Sabodala project area based on slope elements and associated landforms that could be inferred from topographic maps (1-m contour interval). This model is based primarily on RUHE's (1975) descriptive slope elements: summits, shoulderslopes, backslopes, footslopes, and toeslopes. These slope elements are associated with geomorphic processes that occur in different landscape positions and so they are useful for predicting where archaeological sites may be buried. The dominant geomorphic processes for each slope element are: (1) summits—water infiltration and soil formation; (2) shoulderslopes—erosion; (3) backslope—transportation of eroded sediment; (4) footslope—deposition of colluvial and slopewash sediments; and (5) toeslope —deposition of alluvial sediment. Buried archaeological sites are most likely in the lower landscape positions (i.e., footslopes and toeslopes), and surface sites are most likely on summits, shoulderslopes, and backslopes.

High-, medium-, and low-probability areas were drawn by hand on the topographic maps and then digitized. High-probability areas include the toeslopes of floodplains and alluvial terraces that are less than about 1 m above the active floodplain. Medium-probability areas were defined as the juncture of footslopes and toeslopes in valley margin positions (mainly colluvial footslopes and alluvial fans) and alluvial terraces that are more than about 1 m above the active floodplain. Low-probability areas consist of the elevated landforms of summits, shoulderslopes, and backslopes, places where archaeological deposits are most likely surficial. Small pockets of colluvium may occur in the medium- and low-probability areas that cannot be distinguished on the topographic maps, and so it is possible that sites may be buried in these localities.

Figure 3 presents the preliminary subsurface predictive model. High-sensitivity areas lie along the larger watercourses; it is interesting that the two areas with the highest buried site potential are the major streams flowing into the Gambia and Senegal Rivers in the southwest and northeast portions of the project area, respectively. Plotted in

figure 3 are the locations of current villages and the archaeological sites known in the project area. Three of the 13 residential polygons lie completely or partially in high sensitivity areas for buried sites, with another 3 polygons lying reasonable close to these areas. It is important to note that the current location of villages is likely influenced by industrial mining operations, which are centered in the northwestern sector of the project area. We suspect that pre-mining village locations are located either in areas susceptible to site burial or adjacent to them.

Not surprisingly, the archaeological sites found during the ethnographic work, which were all detected from the surface during brief examinations of particular areas, are not located in areas likely to produce buried sites. The strong indirect nature of the correlation of known archaeological sites and likely locations of buried sites shows the folly of designing surveys solely based on past archaeological surface survey results.

This preliminary buried site model will aid the survey design regarding the intensity of survey and necessity for subsurface testing by shovel pits in different parts of the project area. Geoarchaeological field investigations (coring, trenching, soil profile description and interpretation, and radiocarbon dating) will be used to test and refine this preliminary model. A reconnaissance will document the range of landforms present in the project area and will examine the stratigraphy of existing subsurface exposures. We will obtain cores and document the profiles of backhoe trenches and existing subsurface exposures. Subsurface examinations will concentrate on areas where the reservoir, mining areas, and roads are planned. Cores will be extracted from alluvial landforms, especially in the area of a proposed reservoir. Backhoe trenches will be placed to sample representative landforms (e.g., alluvial floodplains and terraces, alluvial fans, and colluvial footslopes) in the high-, medium-, and low-probability areas, spread across various small to large drainage systems. The stratigraphy of cores and backhoe trenches will be described and interpreted in terms of their potential for buried cultural deposits. Samples of the fill of backhoe trenches will be collected in 30-cm intervals and placed in discrete piles so that 5 to 10 5-gallon buckets of soil can be screened to search for buried artifacts. Charcoal and organic-rich samples will be saved for radiocarbon dating.

There has been a trend recently to try to combine surface and subsurface models into one all-encompassing predictive model. We have been disappointed with the results (see ALTSCHUL ET AL. 2005). In our opinion, these models conflate two factors influencing the composition of the archaeological record. Surface models assume that human land-use behavior is related to the distribution of natural resources. Associating environmental variables that serve as proxies of resources sought by humans with a sample of sites is designed to train a statistical technique to identify and then generalize an environmental signature to the sample universe. The major problem with surface models is that they tend to be statistically overmodeled. The proxy variables that are designed to encompass the entire suite of behaviors involved in settlement actually are so intricately intercorrelated that they explain the same statistical variation. The result is that these models appear very strong (i.e., they accurately predict a very high percentage of the cases used to create the model), but in reality have very little predictive power (i.e., they do not accurately predict site locations of cases not used to create the model).

Subsurface models, in contrast, are designed to identify areas that were favored by human settlement but because of postdepositional processes yield no indication of past use on the surface. Subsurface models are difficult to test by any other means than fieldwork. Even then, testing subsurface models is difficult because the time and expense required to excavate sufficient subsurface probes to evaluate the model is prohibitive.

Combining surface and subsurface models makes little logical sense. Moreover, we suspect that many combination models yield a false sense of confidence in the resulting model's performance. Because the training set of sites used to develop the predictive equations is composed primarily of surface sites, it probably is not a good predictor of buried sites; a fact that will not be discovered until development uncovers archaeological sites where they are least expected.

We have found that a better approach is to develop two predictive models; one for surface sites and one for buried sites (ALTSCHUL ET AL. 2008). The two models will be used to design and assess the survey efforts. From the survey we intend to estimate how many sites are in the project area, what types of sites are present, and when they were occupied. Based on these results we can infer population trends, settlement patterns, and subsistence activities. Surface and subsurface models, however, will be of limited help in explaining these trends. For that, we need to turn to from data driven models to theoretical ones.

Agent-Based Modeling

The Sabodala region is an arid environment where in the recent past people have subsisted largely on dry farming and herding, which has been supplemented with a cash economy of limited gold mining and slaving. What characterizes the economies of arid land societies, like those in Sabodala, is their near universal focus on minimizing risk; an orientation that is fundamentally different from market-based, western economies in which the goal is to maximize return. This difference is often associated with behaviors that have been interpreted as inefficient or irrational (LEGGE 1989, 86), such as planting more fields than one has labor to harvest or buying more livestock than can reasonably be fed. Anthropologists have shown that each of these apparently "irrational" behaviors makes perfect sense within the logic of the indigenous economic system.

Another key difference is that the unit within which wealth and power is held and that makes key decisions is not the individual as in classical economic theory, but instead, a group such as a lineage or clan. Sustaining these larger organizations may involve having individuals make decisions that do not benefit themselves. This is particularly the case in stratified societies, in which there are classes of individuals, such as slaves, whose main purpose is to ensure the viability of other classes.

There are a wide variety of socioeconomic adaptations to arid environments. Which ones apply to Sabodala? It is tempting to project ethnographic practices back indefinitely into the past. We know, however, that the ethnographic present has shallow historical roots, probably on the order of no more than 200 years. Nevertheless, the archaeological and historical records suggest that the area has been occupied throughout the Neolithic, or between 1,500 and 2,000 years ago, and more sporadically during the upper Paleolithic. While it is possible that the current adaptation replaced a similar one, it is also possible that present-day society has been shaped in large part from the colonial experience of the nineteenth and twentieth centuries.

We are in the process of developing two agent-based models to help us understand the archaeological survey results better and to select sites in the project area that require further investigation. We are using a beta-version of Agent Analyst to create individual agents, or actors, that will interact with the spatial data developed for the correlative predictive models and each other (see http://www.institute.redlands.edu/AgentAnalyst/). Each agent makes decisions based on a "rulebook" which tells them how to behave under certain circumstances: for example, how much to plant and where to locate fields; what to do if crops are highly successful, only moderately successful, or destroyed; how many goats and cattle to purchase with their surplus; when to sell their herds; and when to move them. The rules governing the model also specify when the group is allowed to grow (i.e., have children, how many children will survive each year), when each group needs to split into two groups, what a group does when it comes into contact with another (e.g., form a village, fight, or move away from each other), and when a group either dies or moves out of the area.

We have developed two "rulebooks." The first we term the egalitarian model. Inspired by the work of Kohler and his colleagues at the Santa Fe Institute modeling the prehistory of portions of the Colorado Plateau of the American southwest (e.g. KOHLER ET AL. 2007), each agent represents an individual farming unit. Each agent has access to all types of agricultural land. Climatic data are spatially and temporally highly variable so that agents are rewarded for planting in diverse settings with the expectations that only one or two plots will be successful. We plan to run the model with and without herding as a secondary economic focus in recognition that pastoralism was not available to residents of Sabodala until about 500 years ago. Each agent, however, will also allocate a certain amount of its human resources to gold mining activities, which will be redeemed by outside agents (i.e., agents not in the simulation) for cash, which in turn will be used in times of shortages to purchase food (measured in calories).

We also will create a stratified model. Using the ethnographic present as our guide, agents will consist not of individual economic units, but collectives mirrored on present-day lineages. Each agent will consist of a small number of nobles and a larger number of commoners, with a disenfranchised class at the bottom paralleling slaves or serfs attached to each noble. Each agent will have access to lands of variable quality. A disproportionate amount of each harvest will flow to nobles with lesser amounts going to commoners and the balance, if any, flowing down to slaves or serfs. Additionally, each agent will be required to tithe some percentage of its wealth to an outside agent (e.g., we will run the model with 10 percent, 20 percent, and 30 percent levels of taxation). Simulations will again be run with and without pastoralism as an economic component; gold mining will again supply an auxiliary source of cash.

The goals of the agent-based modeling are twofold. First, which, if either, model best fits the archaeological record and for what periods? Second, which, if either, model is sustainable in the Sabodala region and at what population levels?

Although both questions are of archaeological interest, answers to these questions also may be helpful in decisions regarding economic and social development. For example, we may find that an agropastoral economy is sustainable in the region but only with a society based on social fissioning and high population mobility. Development aid focused on large infrastructure investments assuming a sedentary village-based society is likely not only to be wasteful, but socially destabilizing. Similarly, we may find that a society based on a hierarchical social structure is viable as long as artisanal gold mining is an important economic activity. Encouragement of family-based craft production, which might discourage communal participation in gold mining, could undermine the office of the village chief, whose authority and power are based on his ability to trade small quantities of artisanal gold to traders from Mali and other parts of North Africa. Agent-based modeling rooted in archaeological data may provide insights into the organization and structure of existing communities, which may prove valuable in designing social and economic development programs.

GIS Modeling and Development

We are mindful that our work in Sabodala has dual purposes. We are reconstructing the past of Sabodala as part of enriching the heritage of Senegal. GIS technology has become a particularly powerful tool in this endeavor by providing the platform for compiling, organizing, and analyzing archaeological data. Correlative predictive models have been particularly useful as means of visualizing where we have found archaeological sites and where we can expect to find others. Importantly, they provide us the means of assessing how confident we can be in the results to date, where we still have gaps in our data, and how best to fill these gaps.

At the same time that we are learning about the past, our work is part of a larger socioeconomic effort to enhance the conditions of the present and future generations of the region's residents. We are mindful that many such efforts have failed in the past not only to improve conditions but have had unintended consequences that have actually made conditions worse. The decision to shift the Nigerian economy from a traditional to a cash basis, which was based on the Western assumption that individuals would act "rationally" and prosper, led to the collapse of traditional relationships and a concomitant dependence of most of the population on government subsidies (LEGGE 1989). Similarly, the development of irrigation along the middle Senegal River in Mauritania, which was intended to enhance and stabilize agriculture, ended up concentrating wealth among particular groups and disenfranchising most of the population so that the country nearly fell apart as a functioning nation (PARK ET AL. 1993). Of course, there are many more examples of programs designed to make things better having exactly the opposite effect. All these programs were based on certain assumptions regarding human behavior and left sponsors surprised when things did not turn out the way they were supposed to.

Rather than trying to make West Africans into Westerners, a better approach may be to make sure our actions do not replace, but instead enhance, traditional socioeconomic adaptations. To do so we need to look back before we go forward. Agent-based modeling provides a means of testing ideas about human adaptation derived from archaeology. We may find that in the last 2,000 years, no adaptation was successful in the Sabodala region for the long term; i.e., people moved in for a time and then were forced to move out because they could not make a living. We may also find out that the only historically viable system is morally reprehensible, in that it requires forcible migration and enslavement in order to be sustained. Alternatively, we may find that an agrarian society is possible to sustain, but only at much lower population levels than currently exist. This information can then be run forward, examining how traditional adaptations and social conventions will react to proposed development schemes. Government and development agencies will be forearmed with ideas about what the land can be expected to produce and how people need to be organized to produce it.

Cultural change has proven exceedingly difficult to predict in development projects. Human response to change tends to be viewed in simplistic terms. If we do X (e.g., build a road, improve the water supply, provide electricity), then people will do Y (e.g., be free to travel to opportunities, grow more crops and achieve economic independence, be better connected and participate in democracy); the bigger the improvement, the better the result. But cultures are conservative, having developed institutions and practices adapted to long-term historical and environmental trends. Archaeologists are unique among social scientists in recognizing the time depth and the singular social histories responsible for shaping a particular cultural adaptation. We have learned that cultures respond to major change not by completely reshuffling their component parts and internal relations but through traditional practices and established relationships.

Development projects that disrupt traditional institutions and practices may achieve the desired economic result, but at an unacceptable social cost. In contrast, development projects that enhance traditional institutions at the same time that they improve economic conditions have the best chance of being sustainable. Archaeological studies of human adaptation and culture change, which have generally not been incorporated into development projects, may help alleviate some of the persistent problems that plague these projects by identifying how modern institutions and practices are related to traditional adaptations, how these adaptations have responded to changes in the past, and most importantly, how these adaptations are likely to respond to proposed changes (see also PIKIRAYI 2009, 126).

Cultural heritage has traditionally been about finding and saving vestiges of the past. GIS technology allows archaeologists to do much more. We are no longer simply stewards of the past; our knowledge can help guide present decisions and mold the future. We owe it to future generations not to shrink from this responsibility, but to embrace it.

Acknowledgements

The authors would like to thank the conference organizers, Axel Posluschny, Alžběta Danielisová, and Philip Verhagen for inviting us to present an earlier version of this paper at the 15th annual meeting of the European Association of Archaeologists at Riva del Garda, Italy. We also would like to thank our colleagues on the Sabodala project, Donn Grenda, Diane Douglas, and Massamba Lane. We want to thank Maria Molina for editing the paper and Peg Robbins for creating the figures. Mark Vendrig of SRK Consulting has consistently supported and aided our work at Sabodala and kindly supported publication of the paper. We alone are responsible for any errors.

References Cited

ALTSCHUL, J. H. – GREEN, P. – TAGG, M. – HEILEN, M. – HOMBURG, J. – NAGLE, C. – KLEIN, T. – SEBASTIAN, L. – VAN WEST, C. – CUSHMAN, D. 2008: Issues in Constructing Archaeological Predictive Models, (poster presented at the 2008 Partners in Environmental Technology Technical Symposium & Workshop, Washington, D.C.).

ALTSCHUL, J. H. – SEBASTIAN, L. – ROHE, C. M. – HAYDEN, W. F. – HALL, S. A. 2005: Results and Discussion: The Loco Hills Study Area. In: Ingbar, E. – Sebastian, L. – Altschul, J. – Hopkins, M. – Eckerle, W. – Robinson, P. – Finley, J. – Hall, S. A. – Hayden, W. F. – Rohe, C. M. – Seaman, T. – Taddie, S. – Thompson, S.: *Adaptive Management and Planning Models for Cultural Resources in Oil and Gas Fields in New Mexico and Wyoming*, Preservation Research Series 5, Albuquerque, 49–76.

ESRI 2010: ArcGIS 9.2 Desktop Help: How Iso Cluster Works. http://webhelp.esri.com/arcgisdesktop/9.2/index.cfm?TopicName=How%20Iso%20Cluster%20works, (accessed July 26, 2010).

GAFFNEY, V. – VAN LEUSEN, P. M. 1995: Postscript—GIS, environmental determinism and archaeology: a parallel text. In: Lock, G. – Stančič, Z. (eds.): *Archaeology and Geographical Information Systems: A European Perspective*, London, 367–382.

GUITAT, R. 1970: Carte et répertoire des sites néolithiques du Sénégal, *Bulletin de l'Institut Fondamental d'Afrique Noire,* Série B, No 4, 1125–1135.

KAMERMANS, H. – VAN LEUSEN, M. – VERHAGEN, P. (EDS.) 2009: *Archaeological Prediction and Risk Management: Alternatives to Current Practice*, Archaeological Studies Leiden University, Leiden.

KING, L. C. 1957: The uniformitarian nature of hillslopes, *Transactions of the Edinburgh Geological Society* 17, 81–102.

KOHLER, T. A. 1988: Predictive locational modeling: history and current practice. In: Judge, W. J. – Sebastian, L. (eds.): *Quantifying the Present and Predicting the Past: Theory, Method, and Application of Archaeological Predictive Modeling*, Denver, 19–59.

KOHLER, T. A. – JOHNSON, C. D. – VARIEN, M. – ORTMAN, S. – REYNOLDS, R. – KOBTI, Z. – COWAN, J. – KOLM, K. – SMITH, S. – YAP, L. 2007: Settlement Ecodynamics in the Prehispanic Central Mesa Verde Region. In: Kohler, T. A. – van der Leeuw, S. E. (eds.): *The Model-Based Archaeology of Socionatural Systems*, Santa Fe, 61–104.

LAFORGUE, P. 1923: Essai sur l'influence de l'Industrie saharienne en Afrique occidentale au cours de la période néolithique, *Bulletin de la Société Préhistorique Française* 20, 61–166.

LAFORGUE, P. 1925: État actuel de nos connaissances sur la Préhistoire en Afrique Occidentale française, *Bulletin du Comité Historique et Scientifique de l'A.O.F.* 8, No 1, 105–171.

LEGGE, K. 1989: Changing Reponses to Drought Among the Wodaabe of Niger. In: Halstead, P. – O'Shea, J. (eds.): *Bad Year Economics: Cultural Responses to Risk and Uncertainty*, Cambridge, 81–86.

MAUNY, R. 1961: Tableau Géographique de l'Ouest Africain au Moyen Age, *Mémoires de l'Institut français d'Afrique Noire*, No 61.

MCINTOSH, S. K. – MCINTOSH, R. J. – BOCOUM, H. 1992: The Middle Senegal Valley Project: Preliminary Results from the 1990-91 Field Season, *Nyame Akuma* 38, 47–61.

PARK, T. K. (ED.) 1993: *Risk and Tenure in Arid Lands: The Political Ecology of Development in the Senegal River Basin*, Tucson.

PARK, T. K. – BARO, M. – NGAID, T. 1993: Crisis in Nationalism in Mauritania. In: Thomas K. P. (ed.): *Risk and Tenure in Arid Lands: The Political Ecology of Development in the Senegal River Basin*, Tuscon, 87–121.

PIKIRAYI, I. 2009: What can Archaeology do for Society in Southern Africa?, *Historical Archaeology* 43 (4), 125–127.

ROSE, M. R. – ALTSCHUL, J. H. 1988: An Overview of Statistical Method and Theory for Quantitative Model Building. In: Judge, W. J. – Sebastian, L. (eds.): *Quantifying the Present and Predicting the Past: Theory, Method, and Application of Archaeological Predictive Modeling*, Denver, 173–255.

RAVISÉ, A. 1970: Industrie néolithique en os dans la région de Saint Louis (Sénégal), *Notes Africaines* 128, 97–102.

RUHE, R. V. 1975: *Geomorphology: Geomorphic Processes and Surficial Geology*, Boston.

SCHOENBERGER, P. J. – WYSOCKI, D. A. – BENHAM, E. C. – BRODERSON, W. D. (EDS.) 2002: *Field Book for Describing and Sampling Soils* (Version 2.0), Lincoln.

THIAW, I. 1998: The Built Environment and the Expansion of Social Dependence in Eighteenth-Nineteenth Centuries Inland Senegambia (Upper Senegal River), *Society of Historical Archaeology Newsletter* 31 (4), 28.

THIAW, I. 1999: Archaeological Investigation of Long-Term Culture Change in the Lower Falemme (Upper Senegal Region) a.d. 500–1900, (unpublished Ph.D. Dissertation, Department of Anthropology, Rice University, Houston).

Jeffrey H. Altschul
Statistical Research, Inc.
6099 E. Speedway Blvd.
AZ 85712 Tucson
USA
jhaltschul@sricrm.com

Ibrahima Thiaw
Laboratoire d'Archéologie
IFAN-UCAD
BP 206 Dakar
SENEGAL
ibrahima.thiaw@ucad.edu.sn

Gerry Wait
Nexus Heritage
71 High Street
Fordingbridge SP6 1AS UK
www.nexus-heritage.com

Richard Ciolek-Torello
Statistical Research, Inc.
21 W. Stuart Ave
CA 92374 Redlands
USA
rct@sricrm.com

Michael Heilen
Statistical Research, Inc.
P.O. Box 31865
AZ 85751 Tucson
USA
mheilen@sricrm.com

Jeffrey A. Homburg
Statistical Research, Inc.
6099 E. Speedway Blvd.
AZ 85712 Tucson
USA
jhomburg@sricrm.com

William E. Hayden
Statistical Research, Inc.
21 W. Stuart Ave.
CA 92374 Redlands
USA
whayden@sricrm.com

P. Verhagen, A. G. Posluschny, A. Danielisová (eds.)
Proceedings EAA 2009: Go Your Own Least Cost Path, Riva del Garda

GIS and the Evaluation of Natural and Cultural Sites during the Planning Process. The Eskilstuna Project

Wivianne Bondesson, Anders Biwall, Elisabeth Essen, Agneta Thornberg Knutsson, Per Skyllberg

Abstract

The Eskilstuna project started as the result of a competition initiated by the County Council of Södermanland in Sweden. The aim of this competition was to produce a model for the evaluation of sites of natural and cultural importance as well as to evaluate such sites and buildings in the area surrounding the town of Eskilstuna. The background for the new model should be the European Landscape Convention. The essence of the project was the combined evaluation of 14 selected areas in regard to "nature" and "culture", with culture referring to archaeological sites and buildings. The areas were ranked in three classes according to their potential for knowledge, experience and utility. Producing a traditional paper report covering such an extensive and complex subject and area would inevitably result in a large flip chart with many maps at various levels. We wanted to avoid this and instead chose to deliver the project on a CD as text and as a GIS project. The GIS project contains of different useful GIS layers for the planners and userfriendly digital maps published on the internet for public use.

The project team included a number of experts; one archaeologist, a building conservation officer and a biologist have conducted the field inspection and generated the associated descriptions. A geographer has done the preparation and analysis of the historical maps while the digital production has been carried out by a GIS expert.

Introduction

The Eskilstuna Project started as the result of a competition initiated by the County Council of Södermanland in Sweden. The aim of this competition was to produce a model for the evaluation of sites of natural and cultural importance as well as to evaluate such sites and buildings in the area surrounding the town of Eskilstuna. The project started in the autumn of 2008 and was presented to the County Council in August 2010. The investigation area covered 203 km². The background for the evaluation model was the European Landscape Convention (http://www.raa.se/cms/extern/en/about_us/the_european_landscape_convention/the_european_landscape_convention.html). It aims to look at the area impartially to find ways of combining values in order to create a mosaic of different priorities.

A major problem in the planning process is the combination and evaluation of different values from different areas of interest. A planner can never be an expert in everything so the aim of this project was to create an evaluation pro-cess model put together by different experts, where extra priority was given to selected areas with qualities from several disciplines. Apart from producing written documents, we wanted to present the process model in the form of a GIS project. In this way planners, experts and public can all have access to GIS layers of natural, historical and geological interest, photos and other forms of documentation. This will make the evaluation process more interactive and transparent.

The project team included a number of experts with different skills necessary to cover all aspects of the mission. An archaeologist (Wivianne Bondesson), a building conservation officer (Agneta Thornberg Knutsson) and a biologist (Per Skyllberg) have conducted the field inspection and generated the associated descriptions and evaluation of selected environments. The preparation and analysis of historical maps and corresponding texts has been conducted by a geographer (Elisabeth Essen) while the digital production has been carried out by a GIS expert (Anders Biwall).

Theoretical set up

As mentioned above the aim of the project was to identify areas with high natural and cultural values, and rank them for their potential to obtain knowledge and create experience, and for their utility. This means that the evaluation and ranking of the selected areas was a very important part of the project.

Criteria

To grade the aspects of knowledge, experience and utility we have considered criteria like preservation through documentation, the possibilities to replace a site/object/area with another, commercial values, symbolic values, the amount of users and accessibility. Assessment of these criteria is done using a mixture of measurable facts and profound personal experience and knowledge of the landscape.

For each aspect the following specific criteria have been considered, taking into account local, regional and national conditions:

Representativity - is the site/object/area typical in its appearance, topographical position, form, frequency and/or containment?

Frequency - is it common/rare in the villages/region/country? A very rare or unique site/object/area automatically gets a higher value than more frequently oc-

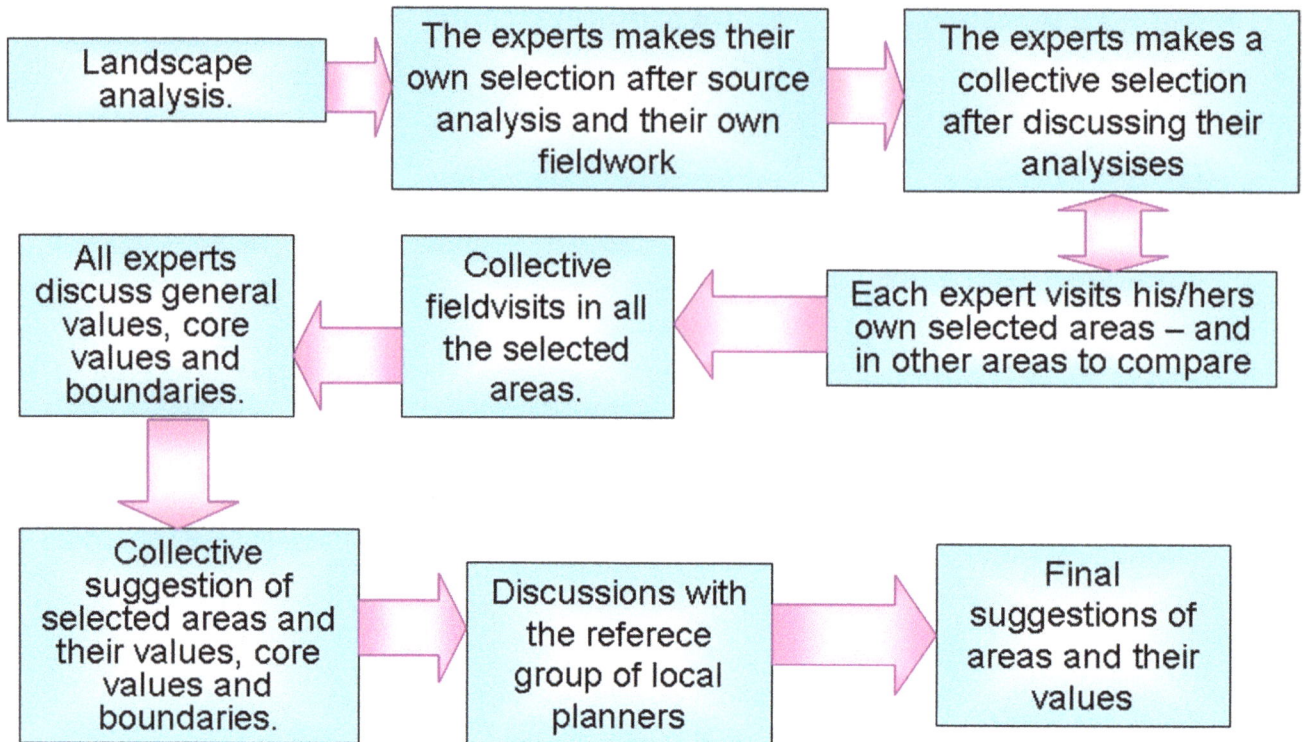

Figure 1. Fig 1. *Model showing the project work flow.*

curring features. Common sites/objects/areas can in some cases be graded higher if they are found only in a small area.

Characteristics – these are specifically associated with the area/region/country. In this case we mean sites/objects/areas that occur in larger amounts concentrated to smaller areas, but it could also concern a smaller amount of more specific categories.

Meaning – does the site/object/area carry meaning in the villages/region/country? A site/object/area could be quite common from many points of view but if it has a name, a tradition or usage connected to it which is of importance and carries a meaning to the local population it will strengthen their identity and create a feeling of belonging.

State of preservation- is the site/object/area well preserved? Damage to features affects the knowledge, experience and utility values.

Experience of totality - is the site/object/area part of a larger entity? Some sites/objects/areas that lack high values individually can together create an experience of totality which carries meaning and creates a feeling of understanding of for instance the use of the landscape or the communication network. This experience in itself has a high value.

Pedagogical distinctiveness - Is the site/object/area easy to see and understand, is it possible to connect it to

other objects/places or fit it into an environment, a time scale or history?

After performing this assessment we then identified and described the most important values in a chosen area – the core values. These values were graded in three categories (low-medium-high value).

In each selected area we then defined specific management goals, aiming to preserve the core values under conditions of intensive use and good accessibility, all in a long-term perspective of sustainability. We believe this is a useful way of working since it points out the important features. It becomes a reminder and a focus on the most significant factors.

The next step in the planning process may then involve confronting an object or area of high value with a form of exploitation (which might imply destroying it). The planner must then consider the value of the exploitation as well. For this reason it is extremely important to have a very precise and clearly described evaluation.

The model

The model applied here is a method whereby a team of experts is engaged, each one chosen from the fields of interest needed to do the evaluation. The essence of the model is the combined evaluation of the aspects natural environment, historical buildings and archaeological sites. This process can take a long time and takes place through

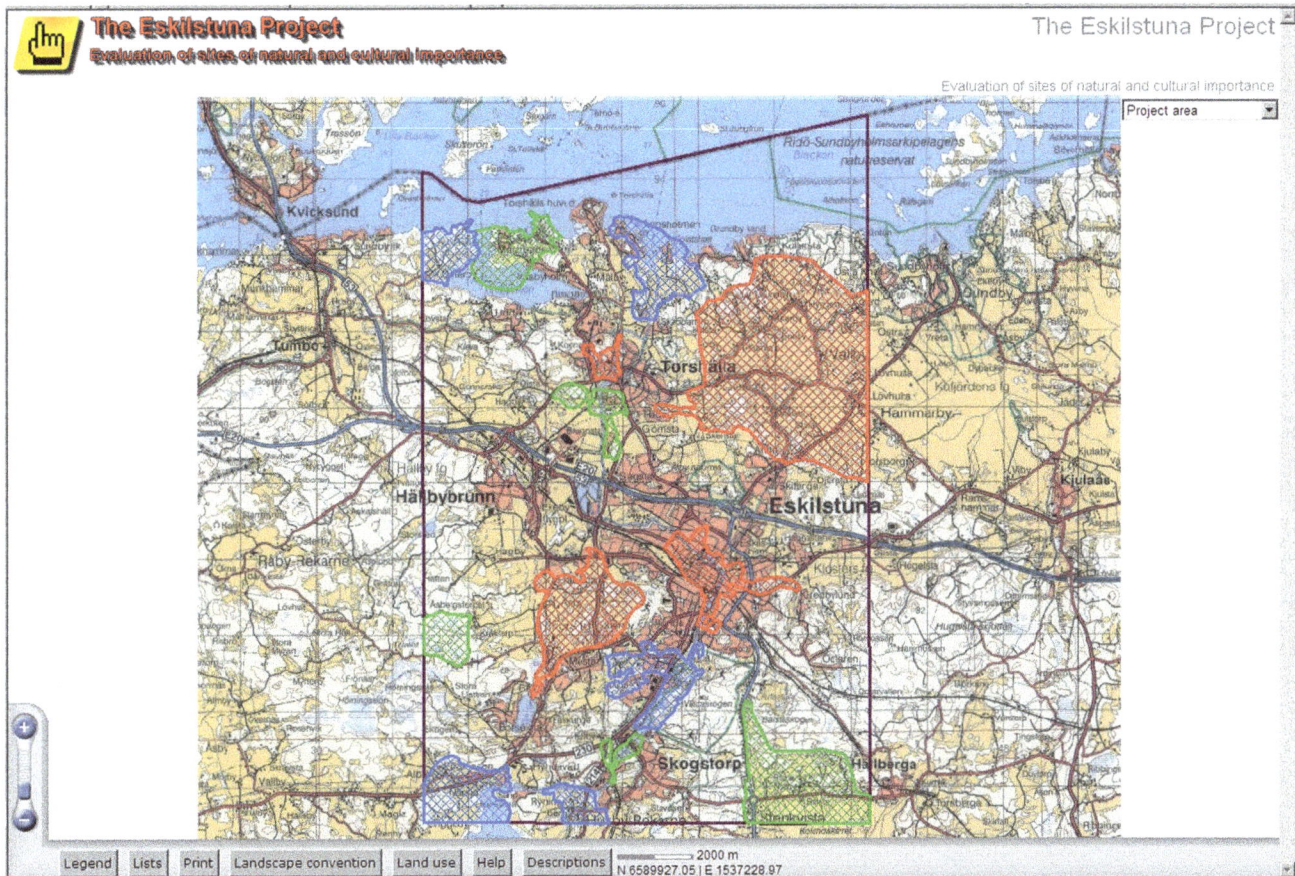

Figure 2. The Eskilstuna Project area.

discussions between the experts. Of course this means that they should have the mutual will to compromise, with the goal to achieve consensus. The consensus should be connected to the points of view the team discussed together during fieldwork. This process of combined evaluation leads to different outcomes in different geographical areas, since every area has its own unique conditions. The model also involves presenting data and results in a digital (GIS) mode. In contrast to using static, printed books, reports, and maps, this will turn reporting and visualisation into a dynamic process characterised by changes and complementarities.

A short description of the model
Introduction
- Terms are interpreted and defined and thereafter used by all experts in the same way
- The interpretation of the landscape is based on its totality, avoiding "small object thinking"

Start
- Collection and study of facts and sources
- Experts do their own fieldwork based on the previous discussions

Combined evaluation
- Combined selection of areas during fieldwork and meetings afterwards.

- Combined valuation during discussions taking into account all three aspects and the chosen criteria

Production
- Production of the descriptions for planners of all the chosen and evaluated areas
- Production of all other necessary explanatory text, making choices concerning pictures and other material in the project
- Digitising

The Eskilstuna project containment

The project involved a landscape analysis, 14 descriptions for planners of selected and evaluated areas, a comprehensive description and analysis of several historical maps and of digital photos and their comments. There is also a manual for the model as well as a presentation of the project itself and a summary of its results.

Landscape analysis
The Eskilstuna Project is based upon a point of view closely related to the European Landscape Convention. In the analysis we discuss some of the aspects of a landscape, seen from different points of view. We pick the aspects that have the greatest impact on our choices and regarding our background. The landscape analysis is an introduction to

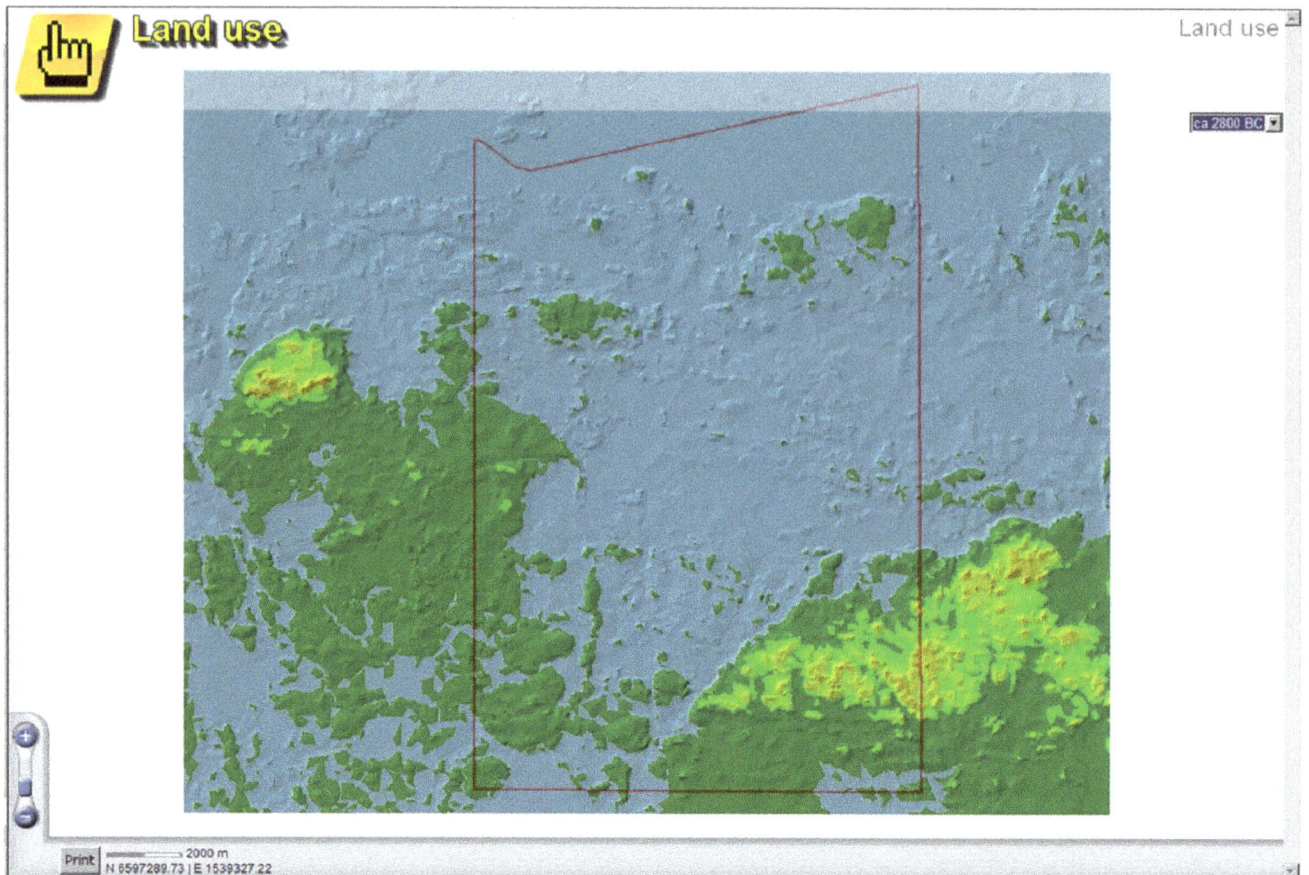

Figure 3. The project area 2800 B.C.

the project – it is meant to form an idea about the thinking behind the choices and to understand the interpretations of the landscape made in the planning descriptions.

Descriptions for planners
Each of the 14 selected areas is presented with the combined evaluation of natural and cultural values, in a description aimed at the local and regional planners. The descriptions are all stored separately in the GIS. Each one is divided into four chapters. The first chapter gives concise information focusing on the values and goals. In the following chapters explanations and more explicit information about the area is given for those who are interested or who need more facts during the planning process.

All 14 planning descriptions stand on their own – they are independent from each other and are meant to be read or used separately. A planning description is the entrance to a deeper knowledge of a chosen and evaluated part of the landscape. They all have the same structure which helps the planner to compare the areas as well as to make it easier to find the facts/values/descriptions of interest.

Comprehensive description of the nature and culture in the area

In the descriptions for planners the characteristics of each chosen area are found. A comprehensive description of the

nature and culture in each area was written to link them together and to point out comprehensive features and processes that may not dominate in any single chosen area but still have importance for understanding the whole project area. It can be read either to acquire a deeper understanding before reading the planning descriptions or it can be an easily accessible source when or if you want to connect a chosen area to a larger context. This chapter is also an umbrella to different articles by different authors explaining or describing important objects/categories/phenomena from different disciplines. At the present time we only have three articles in the project, describing hill forts and treasure deposits, but it will be possible to link more articles in the future.

Photos and maps
Some of the digital photos can be seen in the GIS map - all the others are to be handed over to the local planners in Eskilstuna. The historical maps have been rectified, analyzed and commented on and can also be seen in the GIS map.

Conclusions

Problems
Different disciplines have different ways of doing and expressing things. Getting them aligned takes a very long time, much longer than we initially expected. This became clear early in the project, during the first field visit. Col-

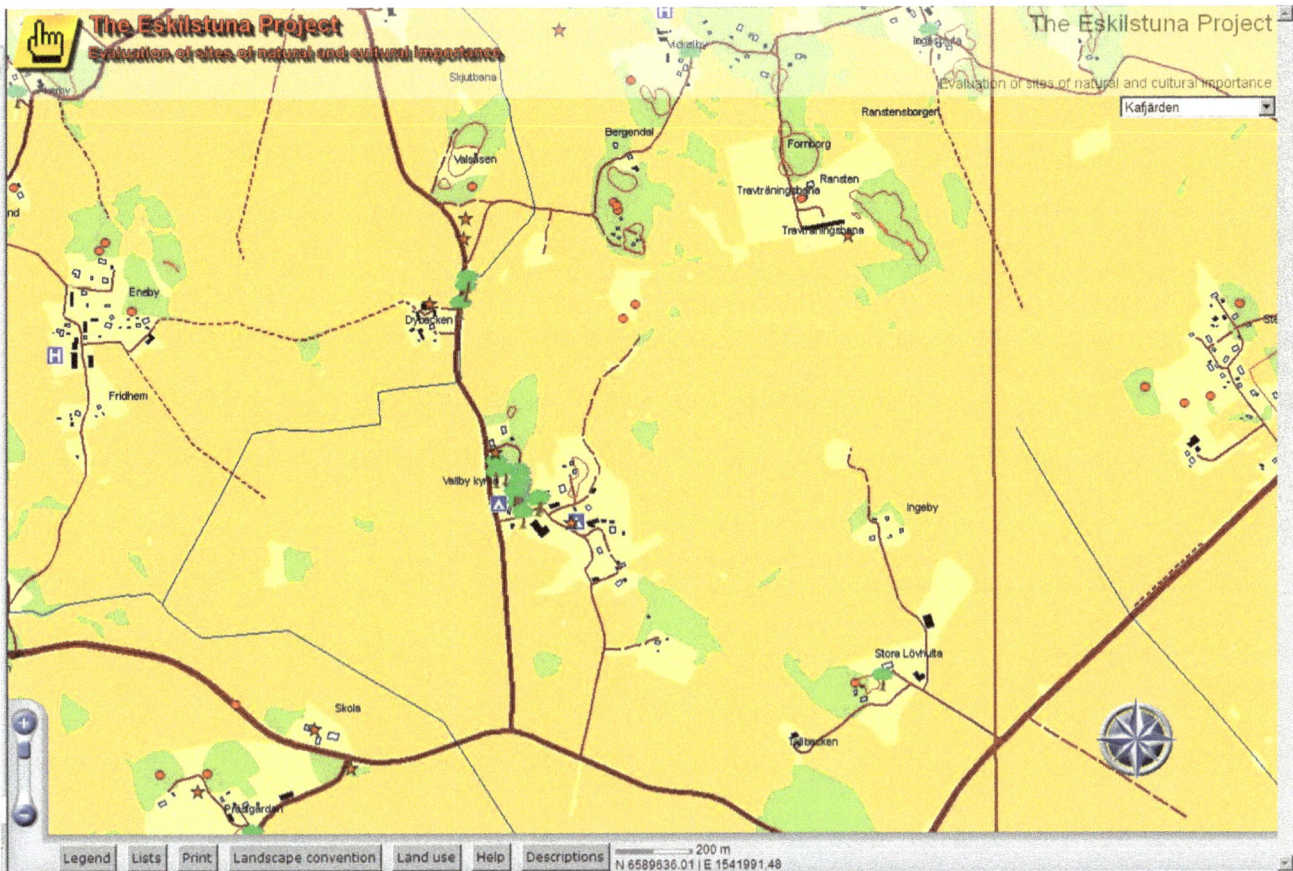

Figure 4. Detailed map with different GIS layers.

laboration improves the quality of the evaluation since it not just implies combined judgment, but also stems from all three disciplines' way of thinking, judging and evaluating. We would like to have taken more time for mutual field visits, and discussions about values and text writing. Even though the consensus achieved on basic concepts and work flow management proved to be a real benefit, we were forced to prioritize our time and money, and more resources would have greatly improved the result.

We also realized that it would have been better to have completed all the preparations and obtained the background data from all three disciplines before the start of the fieldwork. It can also be advantageous to do all your own fieldwork before doing the combined field visits. But this is not certain – sometimes it is very enriching to forget one's own disciplinary prejudices in an area you had not yet visited, and to be able to look at things from other peoples' viewpoints during a mutual visit!

The aim of a model is to be understood and explainable to its future users. It is made to be used. But it is not always simple to foresee which parts will be easy or hard to explain when you are in the middle of the developing process of the model. Some mistakes we made can perhaps be avoided in the future.

The GIS part

Producing a traditional paper report covering such an extensive and complex subject and area would inevitably result in a large flip chart with many maps at various levels, different geographical sections based on a variety of themes, and a large accompanying text. We wanted to avoid this and instead chose to deliver the outcome of the project on a memory stick in the shape of a GIS project containing dynamic documents, from which layers can be selected for future use. The memory stick also contains a complete package for publication of the material on the internet. This material is produced for the municipal website for public access and use. The only part that will be delivered in print is a report describing the model, our experiences with it and how the digital material is to be used. The GIS section in this project has been divided into three parts. Part one consists of a GIS project (.mxd) for use in ArcGIS by the city planners. The base map for this project is the property map of the municipality of Eskilstuna with different layers with different scale ranges, and the map information of the project area and the 14 evaluation areas. To meet the preferences from both the city planners and the planners from the county council regarding different coordinate systems, data had be delivered in three different coordinate systems (RT90 2,5 gon V, Sweref99 TM and Sweref99 16_30).The GIS layers contain information for both the historical and natural environment. Here are some examples of GIS layers concerning the historical environment.

The register of ancient monuments (FMIS) will show us all the known archaeological and historical monuments in this area. Historical maps are a valuable source of information to show the expansion of e.g. a village or a landscape in historic times and sometimes reveal ancient monuments that are long gone. Geological maps can give us interesting information about the soil conditions of the area and sometimes information on ancient monuments too. The national elevation database can help us to build a model of the prehistoric landscape from e.g. the Stone Age and the Bronze Age or later periods. The archaeological excavations database, the register of ancient buildings and orthophotos are good examples of information sources that can be used as well. In the same way we can use important GIS information concerning the natural environment e.g. the key biotope database, nature conservation areas, The Swedish Species Information database, endangered trees, urban green spaces, nature reserves and streams that will help us understand flora and fauna in this area. To get a better understanding of the landscape today the project members have taken photos showing different areas and objects of their concern. The pictures show examples of agricultural areas, ancient monuments, endangered trees, buildings and residential areas. The pictures have been incorporated into a geodatabase as a raster object that can be opened and viewed together with a position point on the map, so you can see where the picture is taken.

The data format of the abovementioned layers are presented in either ESRI shapefiles or geodatabases. This option gives the planners the possibility to combine the different information layers as they please and in a GIS system of their own.

The second part in this GIS section is about how to present all this information on the internet for the public to use. Today there are many different software solutions available for presenting GIS information on the internet. If you want the public to use this kind of information you need to make it as user-friendly as possible. We chose to use HTML Image Mapper (developed by alta4 Geoinformatik AG) for the internet presentation. This software works as an extension to ESRI ArcGIS 9.x. In ArcGIS 9.x you can put together all the layers you want the public to be able to use or look at. With the extension HTML Image Mapper you then put all the layers into a "map package" (for some examples see *figures 2-4*).

By using almost all the information from the GIS project mentioned above we could produce a project web package. The base map was the property map of the municipality of Eskilstuna with different layers with different scale range and the map information of the project area and the 14 evaluation areas. By using data frames with different map information in ArcGIS, the HTML Image Mapper produces a dropdown list with these different maps to choose from. Together with the maps you will find legends, scale bars and coordinates. On the first page of the web package you will also find buttons with links to documents describ-

ing the project, descriptions of the fourteen different areas, the landscape analysis, a user handbook and different articles of interest for this project area. This web package can now be published on the internet and the user (the public) does not need additional software view these maps or documents, just a common web browser.

The third part of this GIS project was to produce maps or GIS layers to work in Google Earth. The layers were transformed to coordinates suited for Google Earth (WGS84). The idea is to make these layers available as kml and kmz files for the public to download from the web page of the town of Eskilstuna or the County Council of Södermanland. This could be a way of informing and engaging the public in the future planning of their community.

At the project presentation for the city planners of Eskilstuna and staff from the County Council of Södermanland in August 2010, they were given the opportunity to work with the delivered documentation. As an exercise, the planners could experiment with different imaginary planning scenarios and then use both the documents and GIS-data together. After the meeting the planners reacted very positively and they wanted to start to use the model and evaluate it after six months.

The issue of copyright is a matter for the County Council of Södermanland who will own the product. The GIS layers used in this study are managed by the town of Eskilstuna, the County Council of Södermanland or The Swedish National Heritage Board. They will take care of long-term preservation.

Acknowledgements

We would like to thank people at Södermanland county council, Eskilstuna municipality and our reference group for all help, interesting discussions and useful point of views.

Wivianne Bondesson
Riksantikvarieämbetet
Arkeologiska Uppdragsverksamheten
UV Mitt
Instrumentvägen 19
S-126 53 Hägersten
Sweden
wivianne.bondesson@raa.se

Anders Biwall
Riksantikvarieämbetet
Arkeologiska Uppdragsverksamheten
UV Mitt
Portalgatan 2A
S-754 23 Uppsala
Sweden
anders.biwall@raa.se

Per Skyllberg
Planerings- och exploateringsavdelningen
Järfälla kommun
S-177 80 JÄRFÄLLA
p.sk@spray.se

Agneta Thornberg Knutsson
Knutsson Partners AB
Strandgatan 86
S-216 11 Limhamn
Sweden
agneta.tk@telia.com

Elisabeth Essen
Krukmakargatan 46
S-117 26 Stockholm
Sweden
senpel@telia.com

P. Verhagen, A. G. Posluschny, A. Danielisová (eds.)
Proceedings EAA 2009: Go Your Own Least Cost Path, Riva del Garda

Reconstruction of the Early and Middle Neolithic Settlement Systems in the Upper Dvina Region (NW Russia)

Andrey Mazurkevich, Ekaterina Dolbunova

Abstract

For this paper, we have reconstructed the Early and Middle Neolithic settlement systems in the Upper Dvina region with the help of GIS technology. Archaeological investigations were combined with a series of geological and geographical studies to collect many different data types. GIS technology then made it possible to combine the archaeological and natural science data to create 3D maps of the landscape of the periods considered and the location of the archaeological sites in it. GIS-tools were then used to analyse the degree of illumination received in different periods of the year, relief features, zones of potential economic activity, and the distribution of different types of archaeological sites. This allowed us to arrive at an interpretation of the economic systems of the Early and Middle Neolithic that is different from the usually applied ethnographical models.

History of research

There has been a long standing tradition in Russian archaeology, and especially in Paleolithic studies, to use natural sciences data for the development of palaeoethnological approaches that also included landscape archaeology (BULKIN ET AL. 1982). It appeared in Soviet archaeology as a continuation of the Russian palaeoethnological school that was developed by F. K. Volkov, A.A. Inostranchev and D.N. Anuchin at the end of the 19th and the beginning of the 20th century. At the beginning of the 1930s, the Soviet palaeoethnological school was almost destroyed as a result of repression and ideological pressure by Marxist-Leninist science (historical materialism). However, its concepts and ideas were passed on from generation to generation of Leningrad (now St. Petersburg) archaeologists from the 1930s into the 1960s. In the 1970s the main concepts developed by the Soviet-Russian palaeoethnological school were reformulated into an approach that was called "archaeological geography", in which the question of the relationships between man and environment was the most important. According to A. Miklyaev, the only method of "archaeological geography" is the method of complex analysis of archaeological data and palaeogeographical data (MIKLYAEV 1984, 129). The aim of "archaeological geography" was to study archaeological sites using all the appropriate methods of archaeology and the natural sciences, regarding the archaeological site and environment as one socio-biocenose. According to A. Miklyaev, "only the analysis of material culture and geographical data will allow us to understand the mechanism of interaction between man and environment in the past" (MIKLYAEV 1984,

127–130). The research tool applied was site mapping and comparing site distributions with the characteristics of the landscape in which they were situated. With the appearance of GIS these investigations have acquired a new means for rapid and effective analysis, as well as new opportunities for visualization of the results. GIS technologies however have not gone through great development in Russia yet; only a few studies were done with the help of GIS (AFANAS'EV ET AL. 2004).

GIS can be applied to tackle different types of tasks and questions: to connect archaeological and geographical data, to observe tendencies of site distribution, to forecast their possible position in unknown areas, and to construct settlement models and models of economic activity of ancient people. It allows us to collect information about the location of archaeological sites and to investigate the relationships between man and the socio-natural environment from an archaeological point of view (AFANAS'EV ET AL. 2004). For this study, our main goal was to develop new settlement models for the 6th to 3rd millenium BC in North-Western Russia. These provided new evidence and facts about ancient settlement systems and the economic organization of ancient people.

Research methodology

All the archaeological sites used for our analysis were investigated in the field. Their coordinates were registered with GPS, and excavations were made, as well as geological test pits. The information obtained from fieldwork was entered in the "*MonArh*" database, that became one of our research tools. All attributes of the archaeological sites and included objects are stored in a separate database. The same database contains the geographical coordinates of the objects. The data on landscape is stored in GIS, and in order to connect these two components the interface layer of the software is used (MOROZOV ET AL. 2007). The program package "*Monarch*"[1] relates the database of archaeological materials to the digitised maps in GIS; in this way, we can perform spatial analysis of the data and discover internal tendencies and correlations (MOROZOV ET AL. 2007). The program package is based on the complex archaeological and multidisciplinary prospection campaigns which have taken place in the basin of Upper Dvina and Lovat Rivers, and which have resulted in the discovery and investigation of numerous archaeological sites. The precise geographical location obtained during prospection

---

[1] Developed at the Department of Computer and Information Technologies of The State Hermitage Museum in St. Petersburg

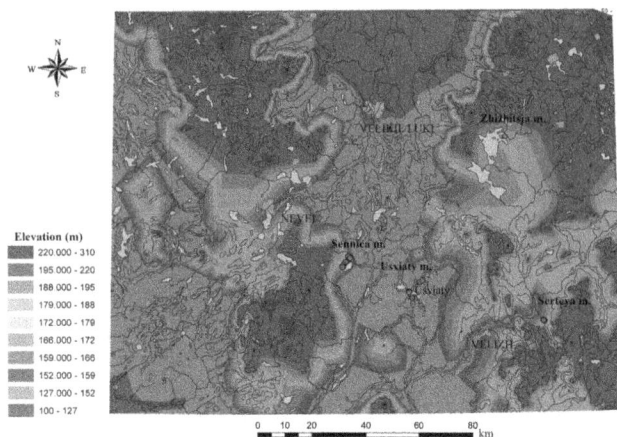

Figure 1. Site distribution in the archaeological microregions of Northwestern Russia.

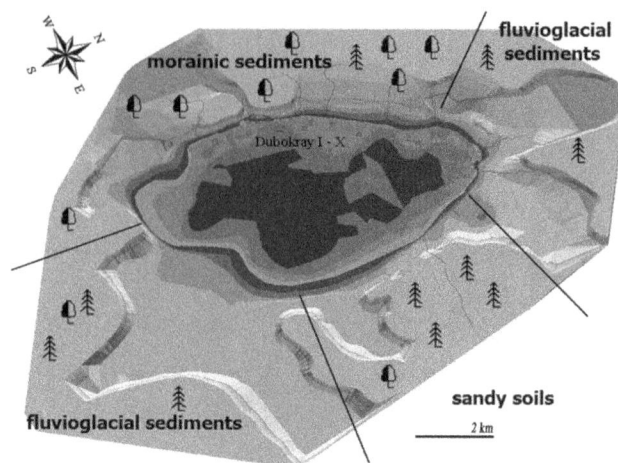

Figure 2. The location of pile dwellings in the lake Sennica (Pskovsky region). 3D reconstruction of relief and paleolakes at the end of IV – III mil BC (contour interval 1 m).

of the archaeological sites and the geological sections, allows us to position them on the digitised map, and to create interactive maps of the microregions studied and construct 3D-models of landscape (MOROZOV ET AL. 2007).

Vector layers of relief, river systems and woodlands were used as a topographical base using 1:2,000,00 and 1:5,000 scale maps N-34. Archaeological sites are represented as dots on the map. Site coordinates taken with GPS were corrected using large-scale topographical maps. This correction was needed because of the incompatibility of measurements made during different field seasons. It was noticed that the precision of measurements made in summer 2000 suffered from the largest discrepancies (see also KOROBOV 2008). Different types of sites were distinguished based on the archaeological material found. They were included in the table of attributes and marked with symbols according to type in order to display all sites according to their functional use.

The investigated region was divided into four archaeological microregions (lake basins including archaeological sites): the Serteya, Usvyaty, Sennica Udviaty, and Zhizhitsa microregions. We have performed spatial analyses and created spatial models of the Serteya microregion for the middle phase of the Early Neolithic Serteya culture (Phase B–B1), that represents a phase of maximum occupation of the microregions. Additionally, a number of maps were developed for the time of the appearance of pile dwellings at the transition of the Late Atlantic to Subboreal period (4600–4500 BP) when there was a regression stage of the lakes in the area.

To model the different processes and map them we have used the ArcGIS Spatial Analyst tools and created various new maps from the available data. Slope and aspect were calculated to trace the inter-relationships between types of slope and site distribution. Hillshade maps were created to show the effect of artificial illumination of the surface in different periods of the year. Viewshed calculations were used to determine the territory that can be seen from ar-

chaeological sites. Cost-weighted distance calculations revealed the zones around the sites that are easily accessible and therefore attractive to economic activity. We also used the animation functions of ArcScene, and more particularly modeled the passage by water from the Western Dvina river along the Serteyka river. This allowed us to look at the sites' distribution from different viewpoints.

The Early Neolithic settlement system in the Serteya microregion

The Serteya microregion consists of a chain of small residual ice-dam lakes (dating from the Würm glacial) connected by rivers. Most sites are located on the shores of confluences and lakes about 100 meters from the main waterway, the Western Dvina (*figure 2*). The relatively modest occupation of the banks of the big rivers could be explained by the exposed conditions of life along the main waterways in the past (KALECHIC 2003, 162). Early Neolithic sites are situated in the northern and southern parts of the Serteya microregion, and are separated by an uninhabited area.

The prevalence of vessels in middle phase of the Early Neolithic could be an indirect sign of an increase in population in the Middle Atlantic period (7000–6500 BP). This supposition is also supported by a greater anthropogenic influence on the ecosystem and palaeo-lakes in comparison with the preceding Early Atlantic period (8000–7000 BP). The water level rose and lake production increased as well. It corresponds with a slight fall in temperature in the Middle Atlantic period that is shown by a decrease of pollen of deciduous trees by 1–3%.

The sites situated on the shores of the southern palaeo-lake (Rudnya Serteya, the field above Rudnya Serteya No. 3, and Serteya XII) occupy a territory of fluvioglacial sediments, hence the zone of broadleaved-coniferous forests

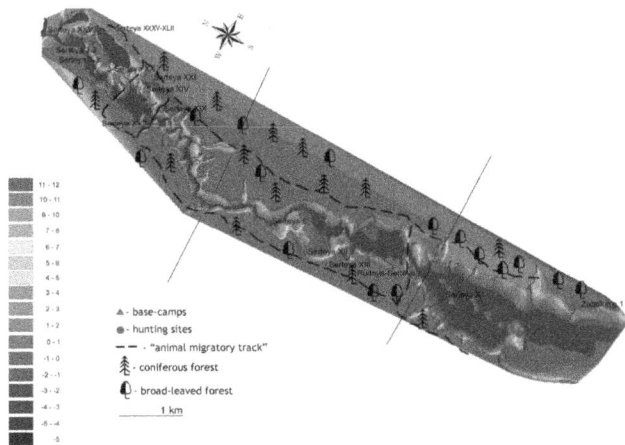

Figure 3. The location of Early Neolithic sites in the Serteya microregion in the middle of the 7th and the beginning 6th millennium BC. 3D reconstruction of relief, paleo-lakes and the animal migratory track (contour interval 1 m).

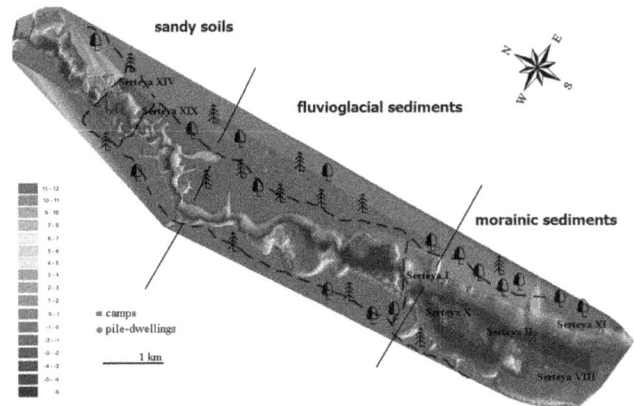

Figure 4. The location of Middle Neolithic sites in the Serteya microregion at the end of the 4th and 3rd millennium BC. 3D reconstruction of relief, paleo-lakes, the animal migratory track and zones of sediments (contour interval 1 m).

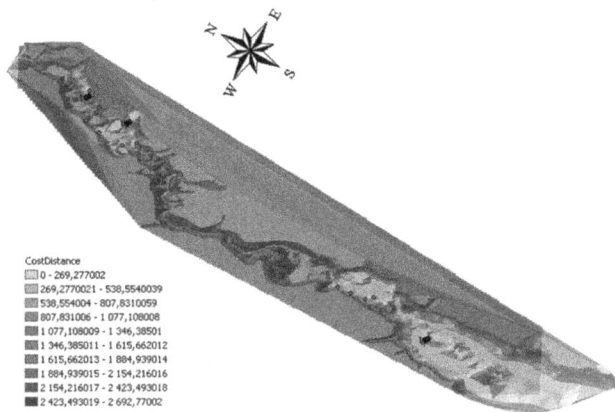

Figure 5. Zones of easy accessibility and active economic activity around the Early Neolithic sites in the Serteya valley.

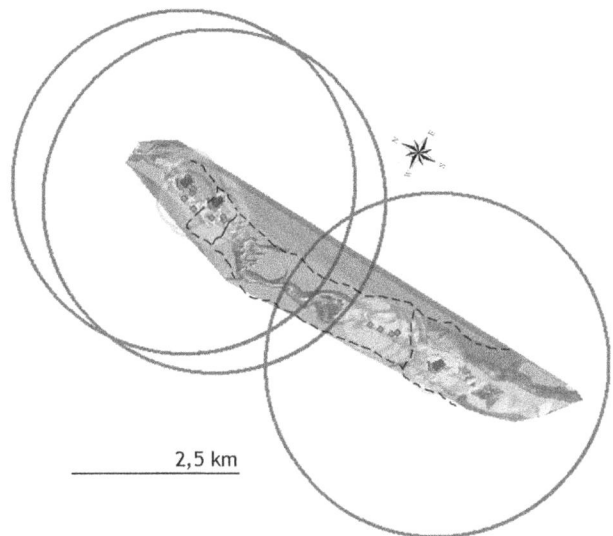

Figure 6. Zones of economic activity around the Early Neolithic sites within a radius of 500 m and 2.5 km (shown here with the animal migratory track).

with birches (figure 2). The site Serteya X is situated on the border of fluvioglacial and morainic sediments, i.e. the territory of spruce, birch and oak forests. The majority of the sites is situated on the shores at the confluence of the palaeolake and ancient streams, or – like Serteya X – on the island. These locations were suitable for fishing and hunting in broadleaved forests, i.e. in the summer habitats of animals. Thus, these sites might be places of summer settling, with a base camp at Serteya X, where traces of more permanent constructions were found.

The sites situated in the northern part of the Serteya microregion (the district of the Nivniky lake basin) are found in a zone of sandy loam and yellow sand sediments. They have the same topographical position and are deep inside the zone of coniferous-birch forests. The surface modelling, taking into account geomagnetic survey, showed that sites located on the plateau along the boards of the lake basins were situated in small depressions, protected on the north side by ridges.

GIS modelling of the passage by water from the Western Dvina along the river Serteya showed that some of the sites that were occupying advantageous positions on the second terrace could control this water passage. The poor illumination, particularly in winter and the openness to strong northern winds made these places inconvenient for permanent habitation, but they could serve as places for fishing or as observation posts.

In the northern part of the Serteya region a group of sites situated on the capes of the boards of lake basins was discovered. All of them are found in a line on the periphery of the lake basins crossing an animal migratory track existing even now, occupying advantageous high-altitude positions. It is known that the migratory tracks of animals have not changed very much through time. Only debitage,

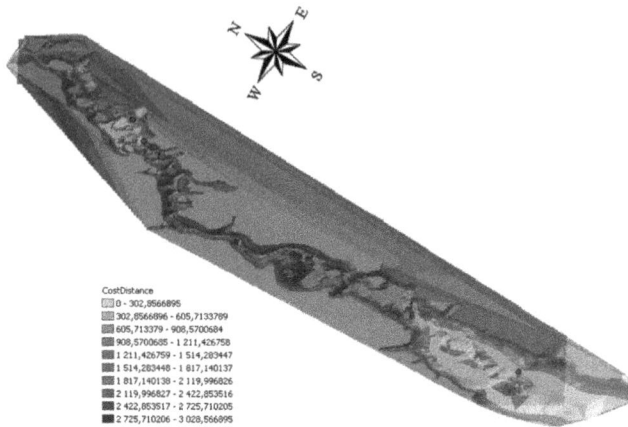

CostDistance
▢ 0 - 302,9566895
▢ 302,8566896 - 605,7133789
▢ 605,713379 - 908,5700684
▢ 908,5700685 - 1 211,426758
▢ 1 514,283448 - 1 514,283447
▢ 1 514,283448 - 2 119,996826
▢ 2 119,996827 - 2 422,853516
▢ 2 422,853517 - 2 725,710205
▢ 2 725,710206 - 3 028,566895

Figure 7. Zones of easy accessibility and active economic activity around Middle Neolithic sites.

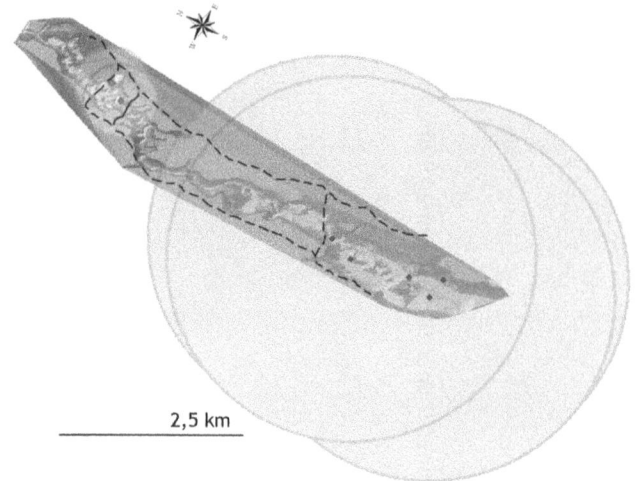

2,5 km

Figure 8. Zones of economic activity around pile dwellings within a radius of 500 m and 2.5 km (shown here with the animal migratory track).

scrapers, points and tiny calcined bones were found on these small sites, Some of the sites seem to be synchronous with sites with traces of substantial dwellings (found at Serteya 3-3 and Serteya XIV) and, consequently, they could all be part of the same settlement system, reflecting seasonal activities of the ancient inhabitants settling in this microregion. Probably, they could move into this territory from the end of autumn until the middle of spring, when animals migrate to and from the coniferous-birch forests of the northern basin. Furthermore, on the Serteya 3-3 site, a three-room dwelling with different types of Early Neolithic pottery was found. It was situated in the northern lake basin and could indicate that different societies (probably, from different lake basins) were living here together in winter. The analysis of clay and pottery serves as a supporting argument for this supposition. A few pots in the northern lake basin were made from clay from the southern lake basin, so they were probably brought here from the latter (MAZURKEVICH ET AL. 2008a).

The human impact on the Serteya (southern) lake basin in the misslw phase of the Early Neolithic was lower than the impact on the Nivniky (northern) lake-basin (MAZURKEVICH 2003). This difference can be deduced from a different density of sites located in these lake basins and, consequently, of population in these two parts. Probably one of the reasons for intensive settlement was the favourable landscape conditions of the northern part that allowed people to maintain an efficient economy, hunting for elk, boar, bear, birds and fish. With the help of cost weighted distance calculations, the zones of easy accessibility that were attractive to economic activity were distinguished (*figure 5*). From this, we can calculate the size of these zones taking into account that areas within a radius of 500 m were the most-used, whereas areas within a radius of 2.5 km covered all economically favourable zones (*figure 3*). The relief should be also taken into account because it determines the extension of the economic zones for different territories in many aspects. Furthermore, the existence of two base camps (Serteya 3-3 and Serteya XIV) in the territory of one economic zone can be an indication

of their non-simultaneity. We can also distinguish two different groups in the northern (Serteya XIV) and southern (Serteya X) parts of the microregion as is shown by the modelling of their economic activity zones (*figure 4*).

This seasonal orientation of two parts of Serteya microregion and the different economic orientation of various sites can also be illustrated by the analysis of aspect and illumination (*figure 5*). It was not comfortable to live on the north-eastern and north-western slopes in winter. That is why the ancient inhabitants chose western or southwestern slopes, whereas in summer they could also settle on the eastern slopes. Moreover, the illumination in winter was better in the northern part of Serteya microregion. In contrast, all sites with traces of substantial dwellings (Serteya X, Serteya XIV and Serteya 3-3) are exposed to the south/south-west and are protected from the north by the border of lake depressions, terraces or higher elevations (MAZURKEVICH ET AL. 2003, 260–265).

In this way we have distinguished several specialised sites situated in specific parts of landscape − winter and summer camps, hunting sites situated along an animal migratory track, fishing spots, and possible observation posts which together formed the settlement system of the Early Neolithic from the 6th to the beginning of the 4th millennium BC. This varied settlement system took into account the seasonal convenience of different places in order to use all the rich resources of the Holocene to their optimum, and took maximum control of the area that was used for the observation of the natural resources, or for guarding the territory.

The Middle Neolithic settlement system of the Serteya microregion

In the Middle Neolithic the settlement system changed greatly: the northern basin became empty, and pile dwell-

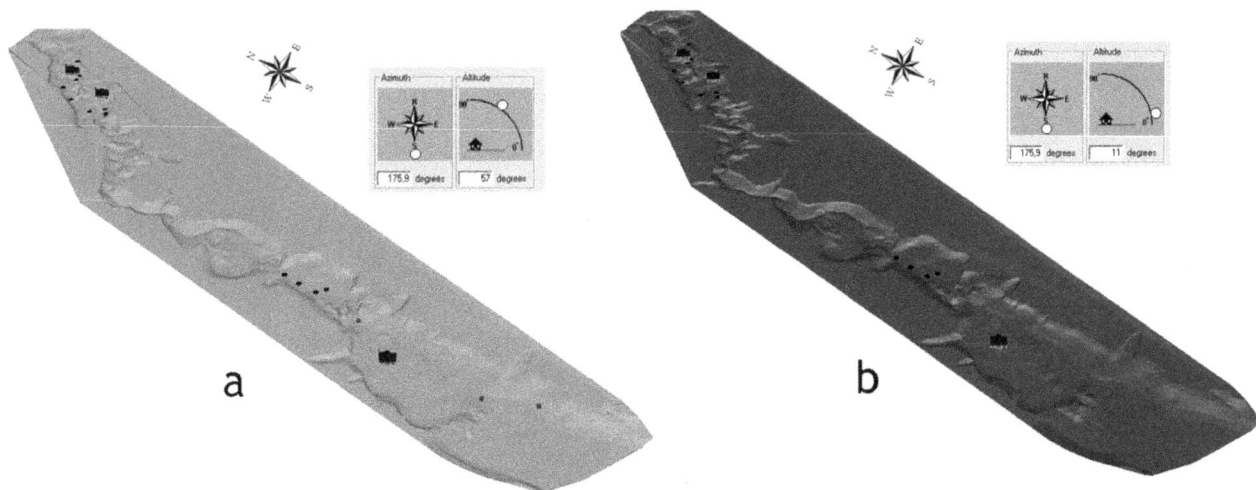

Figure 9. Valley illumination at the time of summer solstice (a) and winter solstice (b) (Serteya microregion).

ings appeared at this time in the southern basin of the Serteya microregion, where human impact increased (*figure 6*).

Pile dwellings started to be constructed at the transition of the Late Atlantic to Early Subboreal period (4600–4500 BP) when there was a regression stage of the lakes. It can be deduced from pollen-analytical data that the end of the Atlantic period coincided with the maximal extension of broad-leaved species, that were mainly restricted to the end-morainic uplands. However, the fall in temperature starting in the Subboreal, caused a decrease of broad-leaved species and an increase of spruce.

Pile dwellings are situated on the border of lacustrine mires, in front of the end-moraine formations with loam soil that covered with broad-leaved forests, and at the border of glacial-lake relief with sandy podzolic soil covered with coniferous forests. In this period pile dwellings also appeared in southern Germany and Switzerland in the same type of landscape - they were situated on the shores of the lakes located in front of the moraine formations of the Würm glaciation.

The pile dwelling sites are situated on islands. This became clear after modelling the ancient water levels of lake Sennica with the help of GIS (*figure 7*), They are only found on its western and northern borders. Traces of several ancient lake basins are distinctly visible in the central part of the modern lake-bottom relief. Several ancient small lake basins connected by channels can be noticed near the western and northern borders. They are separated from the central lakes by capes or islands where the sites are situated. These locations are characterized by a poor illumination – particularly in winter – of the eastern and southern shores, openness to strong northern winds, and maximal remoteness from broad-leaved forests, all of which made these places inconvenient for settlement (MAZURKEVICH 2004). Spatial analysis of the lacustrine pile dwellings in the study area reveals a clear-cut subsistence pattern. This follows from the evaluation of the landscape inside the catchment

areas of the pile dwellings, which is limited for foraging societies to a two-hour walking distance from the central hunting lodge (ZVELEBIL 1983).

These catchments include three distinct landscape types:
1. the lake plus low-lying terraces and off-shore mires;
2. end-morainic formations with predominantly clayey soils covered with broad-leaved species;
3. glaciofluvial plains with podzolic sandy soils covered with pine forests (DOLUKHANOV – MIKLYAYEV 1986, 85-86).

The combination of these types of landscape within one natural-economic complex probably correspondended best to the needs of pile dwelling inhabitants and provided a profitable foraging economy (*figures 8, 9*). It determined the density of Middle Neolithic population as well (DOLUKHANOV – MIKLYAYEV 1983, 186), and explains the long continuity of pile dwellings in one place, as was proved by faunistic remnants representing animals and birds hunted all the year round. The analysis of illumination also confirmed the supposition that these sites were situated in flat areas with maximum illumination in all seasons (*figure 5*).

Site location in the Middle Neolithic reflects the complex economic strategy of pile dwelling inhabitants: hunting prevailed over fishery and a known share of food gathering. The majority of bones found on pile dwelling settlements belong to elk, and to a lesser extent to bear, boar, hare, sable and marten, otter, turn, beaver, wolf, roe and mink. These animals represent a complex of species adapted to life in broad-leaved and mixed forests (KUZ'MINA 2003, 307). Judging from the age groups, elk were hunted throughout the year. The number of fish bones indicates the considerable economic significance of fishing. There are bones of big catfishes, pikes, perches, pike-perches and also small fishes. Birds were also hunted. The hunting for upland fowl (wood grouse, black grouse, white partridge) was conducted mainly in autumn and winter with loops; natatorial game (goose, duck, swan) was hunted in the warm season with throwing weapons. Food gathering was of considerable significance as well: a large amount of nut-shells and acorns, the remains of water nuts and fragments of cockle shells were also found.

Fecal concretions of pigs were found on the sites Serteya II, Dubokray V and Usviaty IV as well, filled with small fish bones and scales. This fact testifies that at the beginning of the existence of the pile settlements some of the boars caught were not killed immediately, but were kept in the settlement for some time and fed with fish. Here we can see the first stage of pig domestication in the area under the influence of the bearers of traditions of the Globular Amphora and Funnel Beaker cultures which is clearly traced in the material culture of this time. Bones of cattle and small cattle (Usviaty IV, Naumovo), and dogs (Serteya X) were found among the remnants of pile dwellings dated the middle of the 3rd millennium BC. Teeth of a horse were found on the site Serteya XI and dated to the beginning of the 3rd millennium BC. The small size of the teeth, the thin enamel and weak painting indicated that these teeth belonged to an old house horse (KUZ'MINA 2003, 305).

We can date the diffusion of agriculture in the Early Subboreal. Judging from palynological data, this is not the first evidence of agriculture in the area. But all the previous "attempts" were not continued, and the first stable appearance of pollen of the cultural cereal group Cerealia is dated the beginning of the Subboreal. On the palynological diagram a high content of grassy vegetation is shown in the same period that marks the spread of open spaces that could be used by ancient people for agriculture and cattle breeding. Moreover, the analysis of the palaeolandscape in the beginning of Subboreal allows us to suppose that the fertile soils in coastal parts of the lakes may have been used as fields for crops and cattle breeding. These soils appeared as a result of coast swamping because of birch and pine forests invasion. The analysis of the chemical compounds of sapropels and coastal sandy-argillaceous sediments also points to the appearance of agricultural activity. An increased content of Ti and Al is marked in sapropel sediments at the beginning of the Subboreal. An increase in concentration of Ti, Zr, Hf and Al is also observed on the site Serteya X in the layers of a coastal part of the lake formed at the same time. This could be connected to soil erosion caused by agricultural activities of the local population near the settlement (MAZURKEVICH 2003a; DOLUKHANOV ET AL. 2004; ARSLANOV ET AL. 2009; MAZURKEVICH ET AL. 2009).

Discussion

The data gained with GIS was used to develop existing hypotheses and allowed us to construct a multifaceted settlement model of the Early and Middle Neolithic. The main conclusions are explained here.

Information obtained from the analysis of the landscape chosen by the builders of pile dwellings gave us a new perspective on the question of pile settlement appearance and the reasons for this phenomenon. The wish of Neolithic builders to keep territories suitable for agricultural activity and cattle-breeding free from settlement (as is supposed for Central European pile dwellings) may be one of the reasons for their construction (MAZURKEVICH 2003a; DOLUKHANOV 2004; MAZURKEVICH ET AL. 2009). However, the ancient inhabitants had to take into account many factors before building a settlement that could function during the whole year. By the time pile dwellings appeared, the water level had fallen greatly and mires has appeared. The shores became overgrown with alder that made it difficult to approach the waterfront. The lakes became smaller, stagnant and eutrophic and the waterfront was only found at a distance of 100–250 m from the shore. In order to settle close to the water, dwellings had to be constructed on the mires along the shores. Pile dwellings could not be erected in the lakes because of freezing-over in winter. According to our analysis, the Atlantic and Subboreal were characterized by frequent changes of water level. The erection of pile dwellings made the settlements independent of the seasonal and long-term climatic changes. Probably, the openness of these locations was another important factor as a method of protection against mosquitoes during the period of maximal extension of broad-leaved species.

Our investigations allowed us to construct settlement models of the Early and Middle Neolithic that differ substantially from the ethnographical models usually used for interpreting the Stone Age. Settlement systems in the Early and Middle Neolithic differed greatly as a result of climatic change and changes in the economic and cultural strategies adopted by the ancient inhabitants. There were several types of specialised sites in the Early Neolithic, and their location was determined by the seasonal convenience of various parts of the microregion for different activities (base camps, observation posts). A specific form of sedentary system developed as a consequence of a specific economic organisation. We can suppose that at the time two groups inhabited the northern (Serteya XIV) and southern (Serteya X) parts of the Serteya microregion in summer. In winter they lived together in its northern part (Serteya 3-3).

In comparison to the rather mobile population of the Early Neolithic, whose economic system depended on seasonal changes, the situation in the Middle Neolithic is very different. The zones of economic activity were extended, the sites became inhabited all year round, and the places and types of sites changed. The fluctuations in climatic conditions and the degradation of broad-leaved forests, the fall of lake water levels, the development of mires and the reduction of lake productivity in the Subboreal could have led to a reduction of natural food resources in this territory and more difficult access to water resources. These circumstances resulted in a change of economic strategy – the settlements were now installed on the intersection of different types of landscapes, they were inhabited all year long and the population became more settled. Population increase led to a strengthening of "horizontal" social links that is reflected in their art (MAZURKEVICH 2003a). It was at this particular time, on the transition of the Atlantic to Subboreal periods, when high-capacity vessels appeared and people started to store food and water. The system of food distribution changed and this inevitably resulted in a change of social structure. The combination of different types of landscape with rich natural resources made the hunter-gathering economy so effective that people could live on one site during the whole year, and the introduction of an agricultural economy was for this reason delayed for a relatively long time (MAZURKEVICH 2003a).

We do not find any small specialized hunting camps with faunistic remains, tools for butchering or "observation posts" in the Middle Neolithic – only the territory of the lake basin was controlled by one group of pile dwellings. Whole carcasses of big animals were brought to the sites where the butchering was done, which is proved by the kitchen debris including a lot of non-edible parts (hooves, teeth, caudal vertebra etc.). The absence of fragments of antler could be the sign of their total utilization as material for bone tools (SABLIN ET AL. 2009). In contrast, in the Early Neolithic - maybe because of a lack of human resources - butchering was done in "specialised" hunting-camps, which is proved by the large amount of these sites along animal migration tracks. This could testify to the different sizes of social groups in the Early and Middle Neolithic. Group size in the Middle Neolithic increased, and consequently led to changes in the social structure of Neolithic society.

Our analysis proved the occurrence of changes in economic strategy at the transition of the Early to Middle Neolithic: foraging economy was replaced by a more complex system, in which hunting and food-gathering still dominated while productive economy had a prestigious character and was not determined by economic necessity. We can therefore regard the existence of a complex economy with agriculture and cattle-breeding as one of the specific markers of the Middle Neolithic in the forest zone of Eastern Europe.

Acknowledgements

NEST № 028192 FEPRE, РГНФ 10-01-00553а/Б.

Editing was done by Jasmine Parker.

References Cited

AFANAS'EV, G. E. – SAVENKO, S. N. – KOROBOV, D. S. 2004: *Drevnosti Kislovodskoi kotloviny*. Moscow.

ARSLANOV, K. A. – DOLUKHANOV, P. M. – SAVEL'EVA, L. A. – DZINORIDZE, E. N. – KUZMIN, G. F. – DENISENKOV, V. P. – 2009: The Holocene Environments in North-Western and Central Russia. In: Dolukhanov, P.M. – Sarson, G.R. – Shukurov, A. M. (eds.): *The East European Plain on the Eve of Agriculture*, BAR International Series 1964, Oxford, 109–121.

BULKIN, V. A. – KLEJN, L. S. – LEBEDEV, G. S. 1982: Attainments and problems of Soviet archaeology, *World archaeology* 13, N° 3, 272 – 295.

DOLUKHANOV, P. M. – GEY, N. A. – MIKLYAYEV, A. M. – MAZURKIEWICZ, A. N. 1989: Rudnya-Serteya, a stratified dwelling-site in the upper Duna basin (a multidisciplinary research), *Fennoscandia archaeologica* VI, 23–27.

DOLUKHANOV, P. – MAZURKEVICH, A. 2000: Sites lacustres néolithiques de Russie, *Archeologia,* N° 369, 68–70.

DOLUHANOV, P. M. – MIKLYAEV, A. M. 1983: *Kul'turnye landshafty na Severo-zapade Russkoi ravniny v golocene. Izyskaniya po mezolitu i neolitu SSSR*, Leningrad, 184–189.

DOLUKHANOV, P. M. – MIKLYAEV, A. M. 1986: Prehistoric lacustrine pile dwellings in the north-western part of the USSR, *Fennoscandia archaeologica* III, 81–91.

DOLUKHANOV, P. M. – SHUKUROV, A. – ARSLANOV, K. – MAZURKEVICH, A. N. – SAVEL'EVA, L. A. – DZINORIDZE, E. N. – KULKOVA, M. A. – ZAITSEVA, G. I. 2004: The Holocene Environment and Transition to Agriculture in Boreal Russia (Serteya Valley Case Study). *Internet Archaeology* 17, http://intarch.ac.uk/journal/issue17.

KALECHIC, E. G. 2003: *Chelovek i sreda obitaniya. Vostochnaya Belarus'*. Minsk.

KOROBOV, D. S. 2008: Primenenie metodov prostranstvennogo analiza pri izuchenii sistemy rasselenija alan v Kislovodskoi kotlovine, *Arheologija I geoinformatika* 5, Moscow.

KUZ'MINA S. A. 2003: Novye faunisticheskie dannye po rezul'tatam raskopok neoliticheskih pamyatnikov Smolenskoi i Pskovskoi oblastei. *Drevnosti Podvin'ya: istoricheskii pamyatnik*, Saint-Peterburg, 300–316.

MAZURKEVICH, A. N. 1995: O rannem neolite Lovatsko-Dvinskogo mezhdurech'ya. In: Mazurkevich, A. N. (ed.): *Peterburgskii Arheologicheskii Vestnik* 9, 77–84.

MAZURKEVICH, A. N. 1998: O proishozhdenii usvyatskoi kul'tury srednego neolita, *Problemy arheologii* 4, 77–85.

MAZURKEVICH, A. N. 2003: Pervye svidetel'stva proyavleniya proizvodyashego hozyaistva na Severo-Zapade Rossii, *Pushkarevskij sbornik* II, 77–83.

MAZURKEVICH, A. N. – DOLUKHANOV, P. M. – SHUKUROV, A. – ZAITSEVA, G. I. 2009: Late Stone – Early Sites Age in Western Dvina – Lovat Area. In: Dolukhanov, P. M. – Sarson, G. R. – Shukurov, A. M. (eds.): *The East European Plain on the Eve of Agriculture,* BAR International Series 1964, Oxford, 145–153.

MAZURKEVICH, A. N. – KOROTKEVICH, B. S. – POLKOVNIKOVA, M. J. 2005: Raboty Severo-Zapadnoj arheologicheskoj jekspedicii v 2004 godu. *Arheologicheskie jekspedicii za 2004 god,* Sbornik dokladov 3–13, Saint-Peterburg.

MAZURKEVICH, A. N. – KUL'KOVA, M. A. – POLKOVNIKOVA, M. E. – SAVEL'EVA L. E. 2003: Ranneneoliticheskie pamyatniki Lovatsko-Dvinskogo mezhdurech'ya. *Neolit-eneolit yuga i neolit severa Vostochnoi Evropy,* Sankt-Peterburg.

MAZURKEVICH A. N. – KUL'KOVA, M. – DOLBUNOVA, E. 2008: Osobennosti izgotovleniya ranneneoliticheskoi kermiki v Lovatsko-Dvinskom mezhdurech'e, *Acta Archaeologica Albaruthenica* III, 139–160.

MAZURKEVICH A. N. – POLKOVNIKOVA M. 2008: Osobennosti prostranstvennoi organizacii pamyatnika Serteya 3, *Acta Archaeologica Albaruthenica* III, 104–117.

MIKLYAEV, A. M. 1984: Arheologicheskaya geografiya: predmet, zadacha, metod, *Arheologicheskij sbornik Gosudarstvennogo Jermitazha* 25, 127–130.

MIKLYAEV, A. M. 1995: Kamennyi-zheleznyi vek v mezhdurech'e Zapadnoi Dviny i Lovati. *Peterburgskii Arheologicheskii Vestnik* 9, 5–39.

MOROZOV, S. V. – HOOKK, D. U. – MAZURKEVICH, A. N. 2007: Database " MONARCH" for the keeping and processing of the data on cultural heritage. http://cipa.icomos.org/text%20files/ATHENS/FP101.pdf.

PLATONOVA, N. I. 2008: „Paleoetnologicheskaya paradigma" vo francuzskoi i russkoi nauke XIX – pervoi treti XX veka. *Vremya i kul'tura v arheologo-etnograficheskih issledovaniyah drevnih i sovremennyh obshestv Zapadnoi Sibiri i sopredel'nyh territorii: problemy interpretacii i rekonstrukciyu,* Tomsk, 84–93.

SABLIN, M. V. – SIROMYATNIKOVA, E. V. 2009: Animal Remains from Neolithic Sites in Northwestern Russia. In: Dolukhanov, P. M. – Sarson, G. R. – Shukurov, A. M. (eds.): *The East European Plan on the Eve of Agriculture,* BAR International Series 1964, Oxford, 153–158.

Andrey Mazurkevich
The State Hermitage Museum
The department of archaeology of Eastern Europe and Siberia
Dvortsovaja emb., 34
190000 Saint-Petersburg
Russia
a-mazurkevich@mail.ru

Ekaterina Dolbunova
The State Hermitage Museum
The department of archaeology of Eastern Europe and Siberia
Dvortsovaja emb., 34
190000 Saint-Petersburg
Russia
katjer@mail.ru

P. Verhagen, A. G. Posluschny, A. Danielisová (eds.)
Proceedings EAA 2009: Go Your Own Least Cost Path, Riva del Garda

Pollen and Archaeology in GIS.
Theoretical Considerations and Modified Approach Testing

Alžběta Danielisová, Petr Pokorný

Abstract

The research project of the Iron Age hillfort of Vladař (western Bohemia) is focusing on the reconstruction of past land cover and land use. Its primary aims are to chronologically and spatially detect individual human activities, and to model their impact on the surrounding area. To achieve this, a multidisciplinary approach is undertaken combining both archaeological and environmental data. An absolutely dated onsite pollen profile offers detailed insight into the chronology of the site, covering not only archaeologically documented periods, but also those with little or no archaeological record. This paper aims to a) discuss general issues connected with modelling the evolution of prehistoric cultural landscapes, and b) find a procedure that can combine both space- and time-related records of the past. GIS modelling of several probabilistic landscape scenarios can be an ideal tool for combining the space-related archaeological and geographical data with the time-related pollen record. For each scenario the relative abundance of pollen indicative for the relevant land-cover units was calculated. Those units were then associated with the particular topographical preferences and located within a site catchment. As a result, the chronological dynamics of the land use can be detected. The validate the results, scenarios with an extreme human impact and those with little or no human impact were compared to the historically documented situation. The approach shows the potential of GIS modelling for past landscape reconstructions. We are convinced that this is a valuable new method for assessing the validity of current archaeological and pollen data and for modelling of past landscapes. It also allows us to gain insights into those aspects of human interaction with the landscape that are difficult to detect from the archaeological record itself.

Introduction

In this paper we discuss the development of spatial models of prehistoric cultural landscape evolution, based on the natural development of the environment and the activities of the communities living in it. We present a recently developed approach that combines pollen-based representations of past landscape dynamics and archaeological data. Our main goal is to show that qualitative and spatial dimensions can be included in the quantitative approaches often used in recent environmental studies. The integration of pollen analytical data in Geographical Information Systems (GIS) can be an important step towards a "visual landscape reconstruction" of the past (cf. CASELDINE ET AL. 2008).

Palaeo-ecological data in itself can never give precise information on the exact location of past vegetation or land use units, but when combined with spatially oriented approaches ("GIS") and archaeological data, we can create a powerful tool to explore the dynamics of past landscapes. The modelling approach we used allowed us to create multiple likely scenarios of past land use and landscape development which can be further tested to choose the most realistic solution. We also want to demonstrate that a multiple scenario approach provides a suitable solution for the problem that these models are often based on subjective prerequisites and will therefore become "virtualisations" of the past (CASELDINE ET AL. 2008), rather than realistic reconstructions. It also offers a solution to the problem that the fully automated procedures often used in modelling allow for little flexibility in model creation (see e.g. POSKA ET AL. 2008, 537) and usually depend on profound knowledge of subject matter and the input variables (see BUNTING – MIDDLETON 2005, 1009). We want to show that by approaching each modelling step individually, using empirical settings, we can easily adjust the variables and criteria used before and during the modelling process. In this way we can achieve reliable and transparent results that can serve as a basis for the development of further automated processing.

Quantitative landscape interpretations and modelling in archaeology

With the boom of theoretic settlement archaeology in the 1970s and 1980s, various attempts were made to connect archaeological sites to the landscape: the location of the sites, the adaptation of individual cultural systems to their environments, resource economy, subsistence strategies etc. (eg. FLANNERY 1976; GRANT 1986; HIGGS – VITA-FINZI 1972; FINDLOW – ERICSON 1980; UCKO – TRINGHAM – DIMBLEBY 1972; STEPONAITIS 1981). There are many ways to assess the complexity of the cultural landscape in the past. Many of them are based on the conceptions of economic geography and Locational Geography (HAGGET ET AL. 1977), and have influenced archaeological spatial analysis especially during the heydays of processualism. These relatively straightforward concepts of spatial archaeology were challenged by post-processualist approaches. Structural archaeology caught a new breath together with the development of the new conceptions leading eventually to the introduction and boom of Geographical Information Systems to archaeology.

Under the processual paradigm, studies dealing with human-landscape relationships try to integrate archaeological and palaeo-environmental data, and interpret the results on the basis of theoretical models. Archaeological modelling is based upon the comparison and evaluation of the structures within the formal and spatial context with

Figure 1. Vladař hillfort and the study area around in western Bohemia

the systems of mutually interactive categories of the living culture. The idea of the creation of "cultural landscapes" and detecting the "behaviour" of particular site types (cf. KUNA 2006, 2008) actually embodies the very theory of archaeological "predictive modelling", where it is claimed that archaeological sites and aspects of the past cultural landscapes are spatially defined, and those variables should be determined, quantified and classified (see e.g. DALLA BONNA 1994, VERHAGEN 2007, KAMERMANS ET AL. 2009, MEHRER – WESCOTT 2006). Today's routine of predictive modelling owes much to the expansion of GIS, which facilitated the rapid and effective manipulation and evaluation of large data volumes with the help of tools that were unavailable to archaeology before.

In addition to the original idea that predictive models serve to protect archaeological monuments by determining their (potential) location, they can also be used systematically to study the relationship between archaeology and landscape. (cf. VERHAGEN 2007; STANČIČ – KVAMME 1999; VAN LEUSEN 2002). These approaches can especially be applied to address general issues like the extent of settlement areas, the preference of individual site types with regard to relief (KUNA 2006, 2008), the spatial continuity of the prehistoric settlement areas, or to other particular scientific questions (KUNA 2006, 2008; DRESLEROVÁ 2008; DANIELISOVÁ 2008, 2010).

One of its basic approaches to archaeological interpretation is the creation of theoretical models (NEUSTUPNÝ 2007, 176). By qualifying the variables characterising specialised activities, these models can contribute to identify and understand the dynamics of landscape use in the past or to indicate its various strategies. By modelling we create simplified conceptions (abstractions) of real systems and on this level we analyse them. This enables us to explore the models of no longer existing or destroyed communities, including prehistoric societies.

The understanding of systems theory is therefore important for the approaches of time-space modelling and the subsequent simulation of historic realities. With such models we can then variously experiment, alter the initial variables, inner structure, relationships etc. Digital modelling is based upon the principle that by using the digital equivalents of physical realities the virtual space is created within which the models are tested and analysed (HLÁSNÝ 2007, 9). Modelling is not aiming to reconstruct past realities; instead, multiple qualified scenarios are created and after testing and evaluation the scenario most likely to approach reality can be chosen.

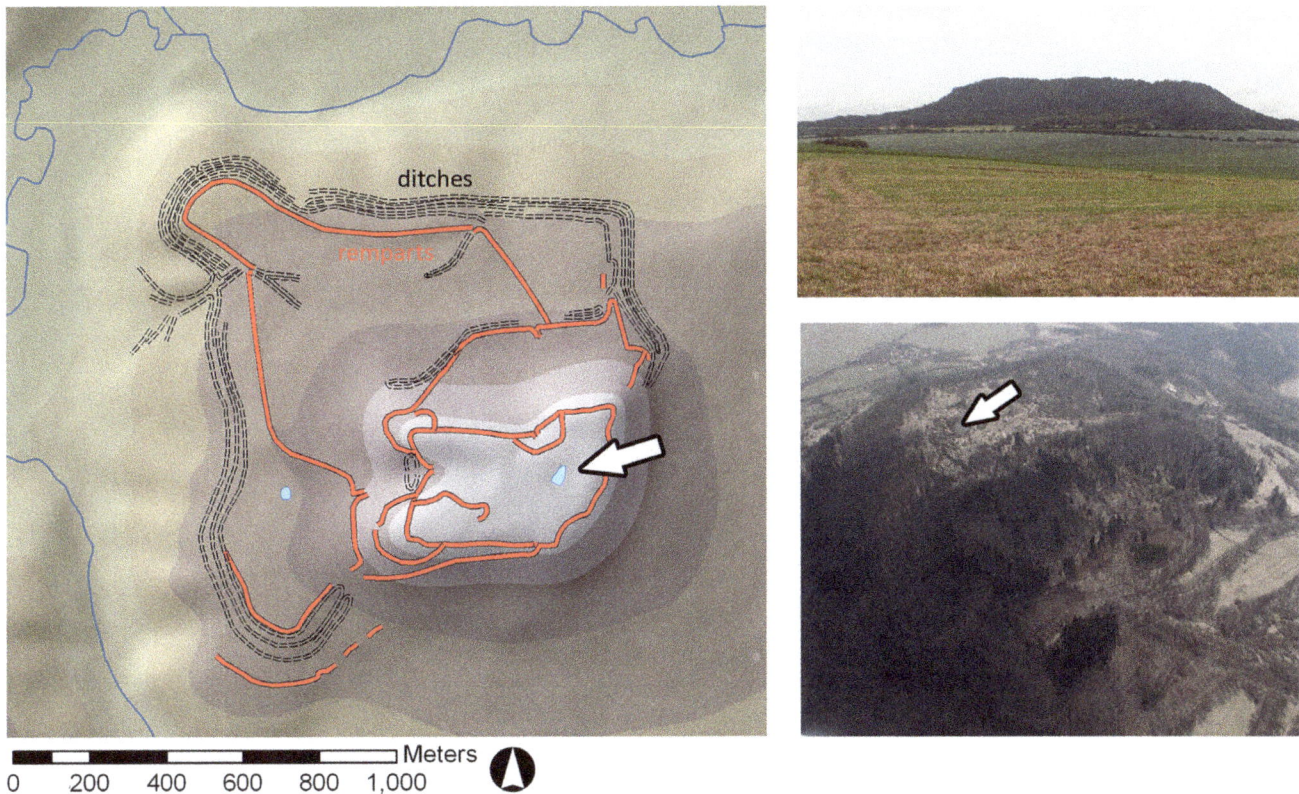

Figure. 2. Vladař hillfort and location of a water reservoir with core sampling.

Understanding pollen – landscape relationships

There is a whole spectrum of interactions between organized settlements and their surrounding environments. The complexity of these interactions takes place on several levels: functional, spatial and temporal – which activity took place where and when (cf. GAFFNEY – VAN LEUSEN 1996, 299). The composition of the individual components of the past cultural landscapes depends on the landscape characteristics and the cultural habits and subsistence strategies of the communities living in them. Reconstruction of these components in geographic space then departs from knowledge of the issue, the state of the art and the ability to integrate the acquired information into qualified models. Stratified pollen data offer insight into the presence or absence of individual vegetation components. Subsequent modelling, using settlement area theory and detailed analysis of the territory, can then achieve different levels of qualified spatial reconstructions (POKORNÝ ET AL. 2005, 88). For this, an intensive dialogue between archaeologists and palaeoecologists is necessary (cf. GEAREY – CHAPMAN 2006, 172). Estimates of past vegetation composition are inferred from fossil pollen.

In recent years, research developments tend especially to the quantitative approaches with particle transfers developed into the model-based reconstructions (CASELDINE ET AL. 2008, 543) developed especially around the POLLANDCAL research group (http://www.ecrc.ucl.ac.uk/minisite/pollandcal; see also SUGITA 2007a,b; SUGITA ET AL. 2008; BUNTING – MIDDLETON 2005, 2009; BUNTING ET

AL. 2008; MIDDLETON – BUNTING 2004; BROSTRÖM ET AL. 2008; GAILLARD ET AL. 2008; CASELDINE ET AL. 2008; FYFE 2006; NIELSEN – ODGAARD 2005). Past landscape modelling can now follow two basic methodological approaches: the Landscape Reconstruction Algorithm (LRA) (SUGITA 2007a,b; 2008) and the Multiple Scenario Approach (MSA) (BUNTING ET AL. 2008, 78; 2009). LRA is based on a model which translates pollen counts into quantified estimates of the past vegetation cover. The two components of the model – REVEALS and LOVE - are designed to calculate the vegetation cover on a regional and local basis respectively, creating distance-based vegetation cover models within the Relevant Source Area of Pollen (RSAP; SUGITA 2007b). The MSA approach on the other hand is specifically designed to generate multiple ecologically distinct reconstructions of past vegetation from pollen signals, forming multiple hypotheses for subsequent statistical testing. The outcomes of the latter are GIS-based and can be presented in the form of possible vegetation maps. Specific software has been designed to simulate pollen dispersal and deposition, such as MOSAIC and HUMPOL (MIDDLETON – BUNTING 2005; BUNTING – MIDDLETON 2004).

Other approaches to landscape reconstruction are based on the combination of pollen analyses and other data in GIS and are much like the model-based solutions. Some of them are basically empirical (e.g. STOBBE 2008), some of them are GIS-based or use advanced GIS methodology (POSKA 2008, GAUDIN ET AL. 2008, GARCIA 2008, GEAREY – CHAPMAN 2006, FYFE 2006). Some researchers have even used the combined methods of analytically treated envi-

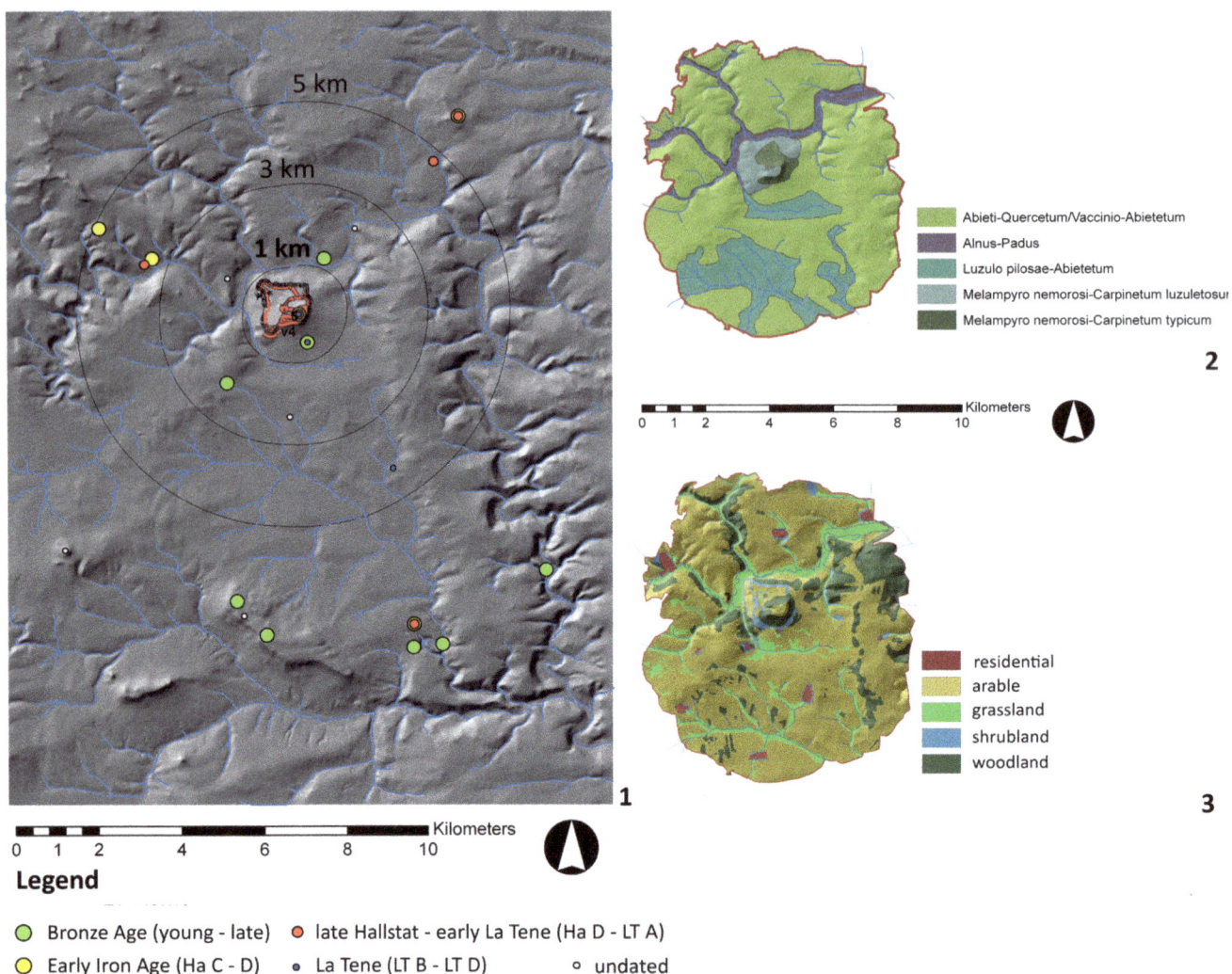

Figure 3. Archaeological sites around the Vladař hillfort (1), initial vegetation settings ("null scenario") (2) and land-use according to the military mapping in 1845 (3).

ronmental and archaeological data in an attempt to explore the "sensual experience" of vegetation in a phenomenological sense (cf. the "digital narrative" approach by GEAREY – CHAPMAN 2006). Coupling of DEMs with vegetation cover reconstructions (CASELDINE ET AL. 2008, 546–547; GEAREY – CHAPMAN 2006) produces two-dimensional arrangements of vegetation or landscape units at the scale determined by the GIS. With additional data the "recreated" landscapes can often be related to archaeological questions (CASELDINE ET AL. 2008, 544). However, experience shows that the empirical basis of these models needs to be more emphasized. Apart from that, spatial modelling of past cultural landscapes should also take into account the aspect of decision making (DALLA BONA 1994) which involves factors like movement efficiency, the interaction of environmental variables and cultural systems (e.g. the effect of central places), particular settlement patterns (concentrations versus dispersion of sites) and the continuity or discontinuity of economic systems.

Case Study – Vladař hillfort (western Bohemia)

The table mountain of Vladař (693 m asl) dominates the hilly area of the upper Střela stream in western Bohemia (*figure 1*). An extensive fortification system encloses an area of 115 ha and includes the extent of the adjacent foothills as well (*figure 2*). Recent excavations have shown that the fortification system has a long and complex history with at least five construction phases, the oldest coming from the Bronze Age and the latest dating probably to the Late La Tène period (CHYTRÁČEK – ŠMEJDA 2005). The hillfort had an important position within the inter-regional contacts especially during the Late Hallstatt – Early La Tène periods, when the size and occupation density of the site reached its maximum. The importance of the hillfort and its location can probably be attributed to the rich gold-bearing areas existing in the vicinity (CHYTRÁČEK – ŠMEJDA 2005, 5–6). The site however does not appear to be a typical representative of the contemporary *Fürstensitze*-sites ("Princely Sites") known from the Western Hallstatt regions. Despite the evident Late La Tène occupation, the site probably did not function as a typical oppidum either. It seems that it was an independent central place in its

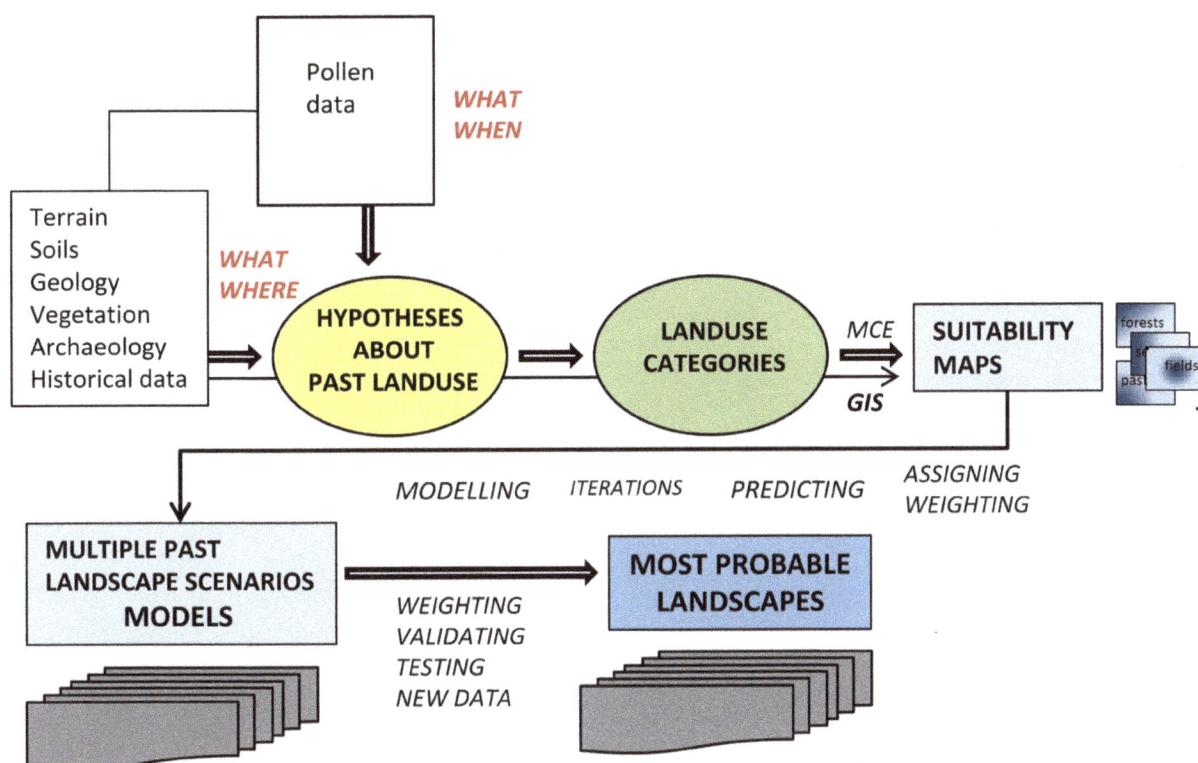

Figure 4. Schematic representation of the workflow.

region, outside the socio-political systems developing in central and southern Bohemia which led to the growth and subsequent fall of the oppida.

The Vladař hillfort settlement saw its peak during the beginning of the La Tène period. Occupation started to decline by the end of 3rd century BC, and the site was completely abandoned around the verge of a century after which it reverted back to natural woodland (POKORNÝ ET AL. 2006). It was again settled for a brief period during the Early Middle Ages, and from the Medieval period onward the area started to be used for agriculture. This situation continued until the mid 20th century, and now the site is again covered by shrubs and expanding woodland (*figure 2*). These conclusions are mainly drawn from palaeo-environmental research; the archaeological data remains mostly fragmentary and discontinuous. The hillfort of Vladař offers ideal conditions for modern palaeo-environmental research because of a rather exceptional combination of archaeological and palaeo-ecological evidence (POKORNÝ ET AL. 2006). First of all, it offers a unique opportunity to study a continuous sedimentary record from the peat deposits in the original cistern which was built right at the centre of the acropolis (*figure 2*) around 400 BC. In 2004 a continuous sedimentary record of a basin was sampled (POKORNÝ ET AL. 2005) and offered the first opportunity ever in the Czech Republic to examine the development of a prehistoric hillfort on the basis of direct and highly

detailed botanical indices with high chronological accuracy. In this way, a detailed insight in the site's chronology was obtained and human occupation could even be proved during periods with little or no archaeological evidence. It also documented the events connected to the site's abandonment and the following vegetational succession from settlement to natural forest (POKORNÝ ET AL. 2006, 420).

Modelling approach

The ongoing research project of the hillfort of Vladař and the surrounding region is, among others, concerned with the reconstruction of the development of the cultural landscape, past vegetation and land-use around the site and within its fortifications. There can be no doubt that the settlement area of such an extensive hillfort contained all the essential elements of a prehistoric cultural landscape: a central settlement; associated villages in the vicinity (as proven by surface artefact studies); agricultural land (fields, fallow, pastures, and meadows); transitional zones of woodland managed for grazing, bedding and coppicing; probably forest of a more or less natural composition and structure; and areas for production, burial, ritual, and assembly. The changes in the pollen assemblages reflect the changes in human impact on the site and its surroundings with respect to secondary woodland composition, use of crops, intensity of pasture, and the vegetation composition

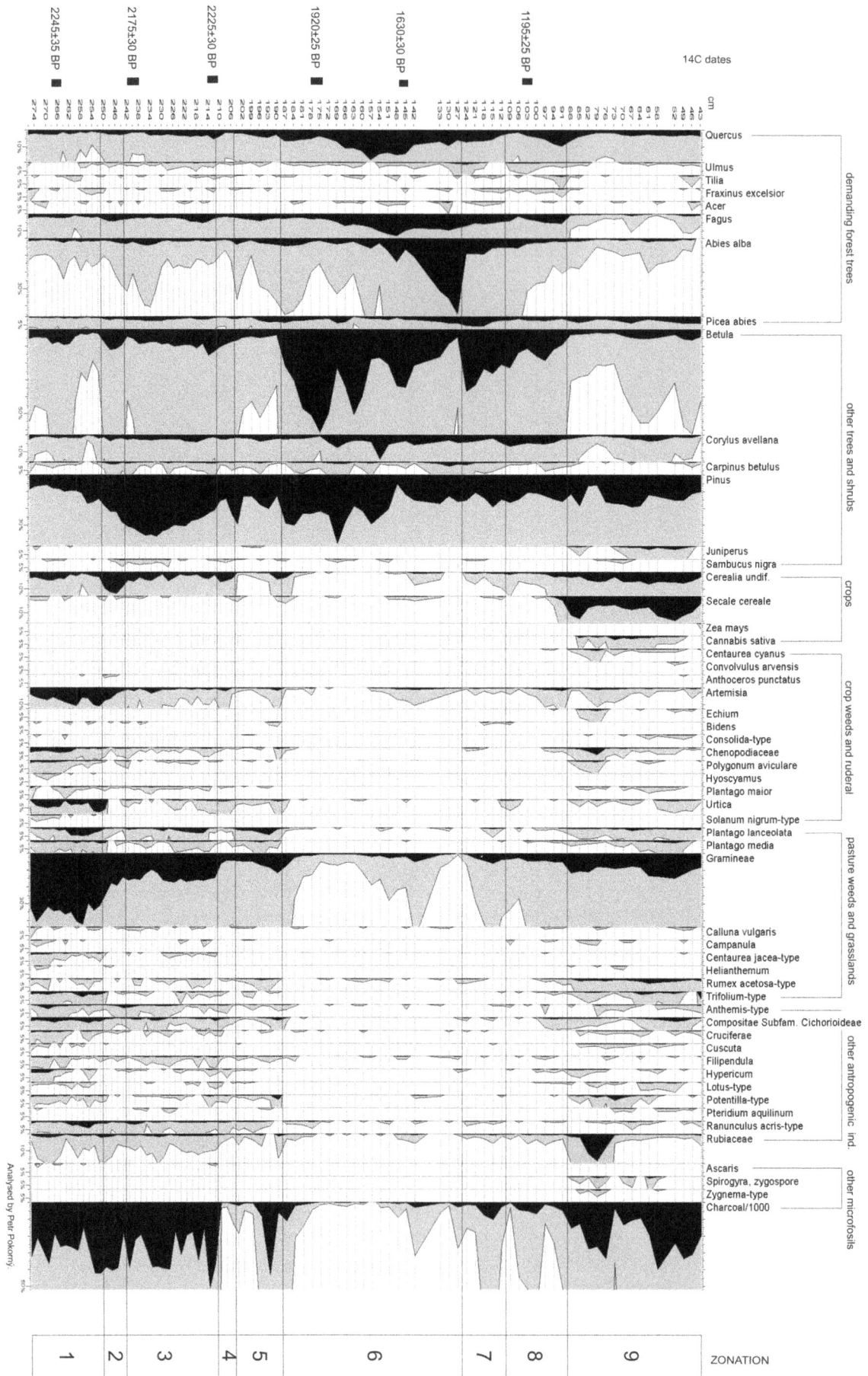

Figure 5. Percentage pollen diagram made from sediments of the cistern located at Vladař hillfort acropolis. Only selected taxa are shown.

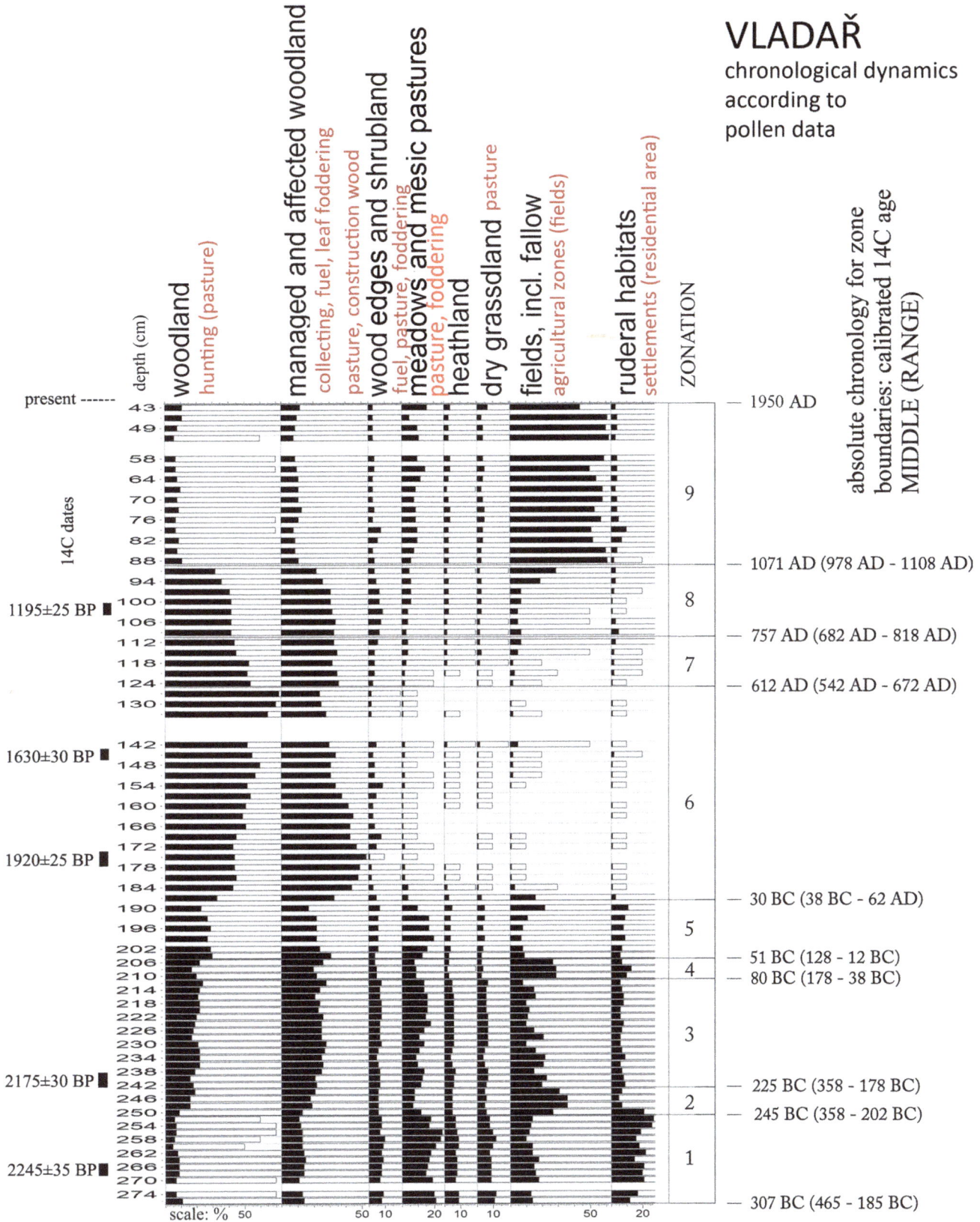

Figure 6. Pollen diagram. Succession of habitats according to pollen data.

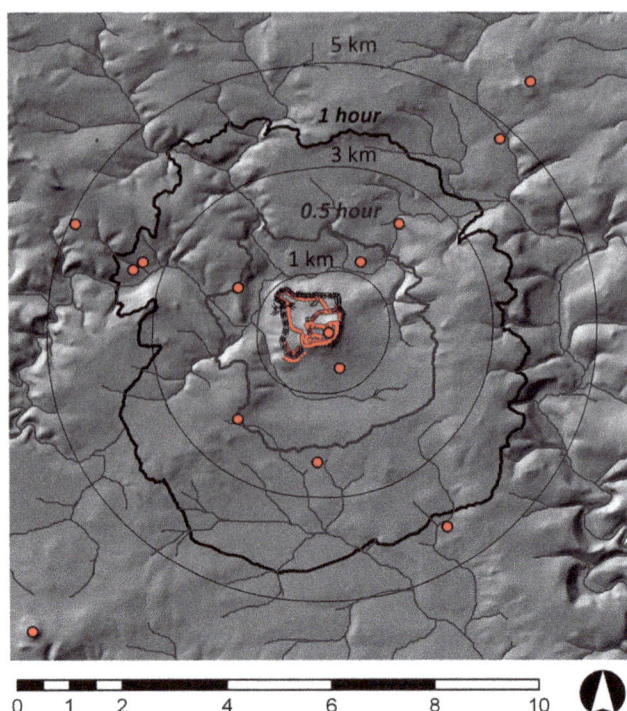

Figure 7. Test area around the hillfort of Vladař and the one ("1 hour") considered as basis for the relevant extent for the pollen dispersal and land-use modelling.

of settlement areas (POKORNÝ ET AL. 2006, 420). The primary aims of this project are to detect the particular human activities during the time of the site's occupation, their extent and localisation within a particular site catchment and to model their impact on vegetation cover diversity and successive processes in the surrounding landscape.

time-related pollen records, and map the dynamics of vegetation cover and land use change, is by using GIS-modelling of probabilistic cultural landscape scenarios within a projected site catchment (based on pollen dispersal and cost surface models; see below). A single pollen profile located in the very centre of the hillfort offers high-resolution pollen-analytical data with continuous sedimentation from ca. 300 BC up to the present. As a result, the temporal dynamics of land use can be detected, distunguishing periods with an extreme human impact (occurring during the Early La Tène period, and gradually from the post-Medieval period onward, see figures 5 and 6), and periods with little or no human impact compared to the external evidence represented by the "null scenario" (the modelled "initial stage" with no human impact), using the 19th century and present day landscape scenarios as validation (figure 3). The combination of archaeological and pollen data is an uncommon approach, because the usual methods of palaeo-environmental reconstruction do not include the actual archaeological record or record of past habitation. Archaeological data can in this case also be used as the independent external line of evidence which can correlate the spatial aspects of the environmental data. Archaeological evidence from the area shows that from the beginning of the sedimentation in the cistern in the acropolis in the 4th century BC there was no contemporary open settlement in the surrounding area. All the available occupation evidence is dated to the Late Bronze Age or the Hallstatt Period (figure 3) and we can assume that during the existence of the cistern at the acropolis settlement activities were limited to the hillfort and its close vicinity.

zone number	Zone chronology	woodland	managed and affected woodland	wood edges and shrubland	meadows and pastures	mesic grasslands	heathland	fields including fallow	ruderal habitats	%
zone 9	1071-2000 AD	8	10	4	10	4	3	56	4	
zone 8	757-1071 AD	39	30	7	5	3	2	11	3	
zone 7	612-757 AD	50	34	4	3	2	2	4	2	
zone 6	31 BC-612 AD	52	38	4	2	1	1	2	1	
zone 5	51-30 BC	28	23	6	16	5	4	11	8	100
zone 4	80-51 BC	20	22	5	9	3	3	28	10	
zone 3	225-80 BC	20	25	7	14	6	6	15	7	

Table 1. Chronological zoning of the profile and quantitative representation of the landscape units (categories).

To achieve this, a multidisciplinary approach is undertaken integrating both archaeological and environmental data with GIS-based analytical tools, in order to create a set of chronologically distinctive landscape models based on the data from a single onsite pollen profile. The data concerning landscape morphology, geology, soil cover and climate were combined with data on past occupation (based on archaeological excavations and surface survey) and past vegetation (based on the results of pollen analyses). The greatest problem we faced for this analysis is the fact that pollen data is not spatially determined, unlike the rest. When we only dispose of a single pollen profile, the spatial interpretation of these data remains obscure. The best method to combine the spatially related data with the

The workflow we used is outlined below (figure 4) and involves a series of stages. The basic premise of the approach was to combine empirical data and quantitative analytical tools; for this, we had to limit automated data processing and employ a transparent framework for each modelling step. This allowed to retrace the procedure at any time during the modelling process.

The pollen profile was divided into 9 time-transgressive slices, homogenous in vegetation character (figure 5 and 6). Boundaries between the slice were placed at key break points in land cover development, in the same way pollen analysts usually delimit Local Pollen Assemblage Zones. For each time slice, the relative abundance of pollen in-

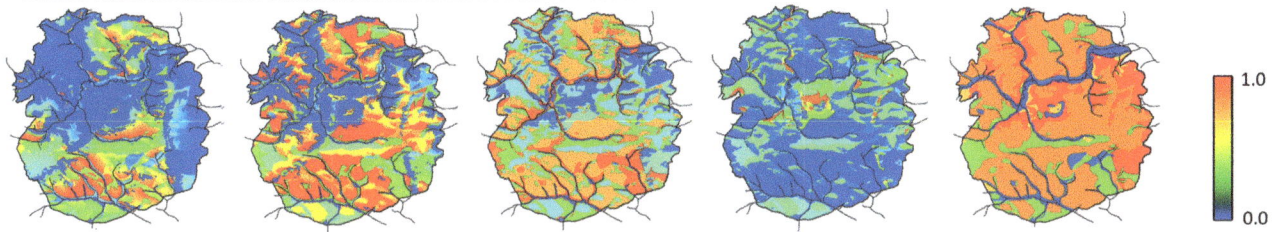

Figure 8. Suitability maps for the individual land-cover units.

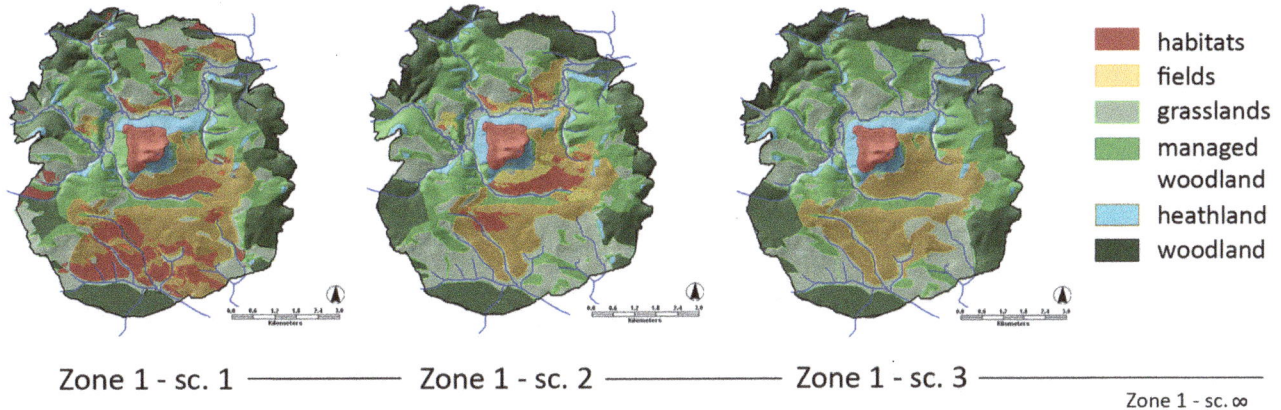

Zone 1 - sc. 1 ————— Zone 1 - sc. 2 ————— Zone 1 - sc. 3 —————

Zone 1 - sc. ∞

Figure 9. Options for the possible scenarios of the Zone 1 representing namely the distance weighting of the pollen dispersal and the spread versus intensity criteria for settlement activities.

dicative for the relevant vegetation groupings of individual land cover units was calculated.

The following land cover categories were chosen:
a) woodland,
b) managed and affected woodland,
c) wood edges and shrubland,
d) meadows and mesic
e) pastures,
f) heathland,
g) dry grassland,
h) fields (including fallow),
i) ruderal habitats.

The recalculation of raw pollen percentages into quantitative estimates of land cover unit occurrence was based on empirical estimates of pollen productivity on a scale from 1 (least productive) to 5 (maximum productivity), and ecological indicator values of individual pollen types in respect to certain vegetation categories on a scale of 0 (no occurrence in respective type of vegetation) to 5 (strong affinity to respective type of vegetation). The calculated proportions of the land cover units (*table 1*) were then associated with their particular topographical preferences and positioned within a site catchment according to pollen dispersion and the other criteria (see below).

Isolated time slices represent individual points in time – these are the "land use scenarios" which are meant to be stacked chronologically in order to visualize the cultural

landscape dynamics in space and time. The main problem with this approach is the (wrong) assumption that land use was constant in time.

The ultimate question to be solved is the detection of the relevant spatial extent for the model; many models rely on calculated RSAP (cf. SUGITA ET AL. 2007b; BROSTRÖM ET AL. 2005; BUNTING ET AL. 2008, 78; CASELDINE ET AL. 2008, 543, 545 etc.). The extent needs to be determined on the basis on number of criteria – especially pollen dispersal estimates across a three-dimensional landscape (relief) and settlement area theory. The actual model area for this project was inferred from the current state of vegetation within the cistern (where the pollen profile was sampled) during the particular time slices and combined with the movement costs across the landscape up to a distance of 5 km: one walking hour for open pond, one half for partially weedy, 15 minutes (or one kilometre) for marsh (*figure 7*). This approach was accepted especially because we tend to model the cultural landscape with communities living and moving in it.

The identification of specific topographical units (edges, individual parts of slopes, channels, ridges etc.) in the landscape was done using topographic variables (slope, aspect, longitudinal curvature, topographic and movement costs, distance to water streams) and was completed by information on soils, geology and reconstructed natural vegetation. Identified and isolated units were then associated with specified land use categories and the suitability

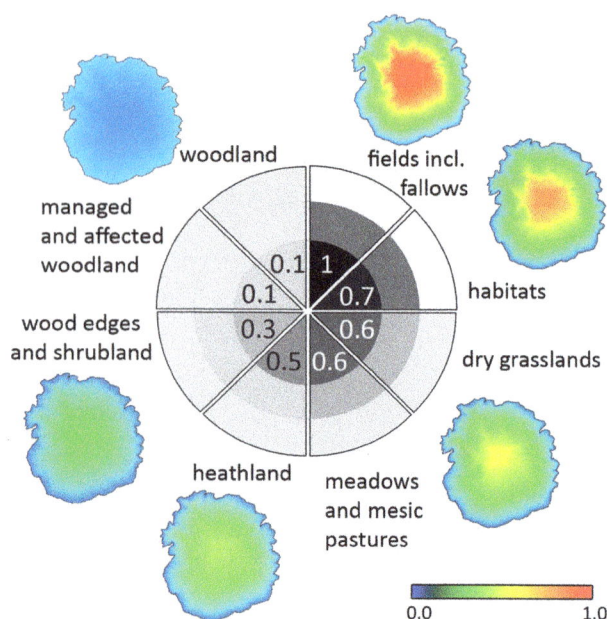

Figure 10. Weights used for the impact on pollen dispersal and its affection on models.

maps for each single category – settlements, fields (including fallow), grasslands (all the grasslands were considered as one category in this initial phase), heathlands, woodlands – were created (*figure 8*). Not all variables used for the suitability maps have the same impact. Therefore, the weighted values method of the Multi Criteria Evaluation (MCE) tool in IDRISI was applied, because it works with contextual parameters by taking into account several descriptors at once. Multi Criteria Evaluation is a decision support tool (cf. EASTMAN 2006, 87, 126–134) providing choices between multiple alternatives based on sets of criteria which could either support or limit the decision. Here the goal was to combine a set of differently weighted criteria to achieve a single composite basis for making suitability maps. In this way it is possible to appreciate and integrate the complexity of the past landscapes. The resulting suitability maps then had to be reclassified in order to achieve a unique dispersion of values (from 0 to 1 using the Rank operation) for subsequent use in modelling.

Based on the previous steps, we then modelled multiple possible land use scenarios (for a description of the concept see BUNTING ET AL. 2008, BUNTING – MIDDLETON 2009). Our approach is based on the fact that different landscapes can produce the same pollen signal, so there is a need for defining multiple possibilities in the form of probabilistic landscape scenarios (BUNTING – MIDDLETON 2009, 800). In this case the generation of multiple possible scenarios was not automated through the specified software, but was done on the basis of the approaches processed in GIS. Our multiple possible land-use scenarios (for an example see *figure 9*) visualize several models of one landscape in a particular time slot based on suitability maps (incorporating the physical environment parameters) and quantitative proportions of the land use categories (*table 1*), and also

taking into account factors like settlement area theory and cultural variables (archaeological evidence, movement costs, spatial extent versus intensity of activities). To generate these scenarios, iterative functions and macro building operations had to be developed and several procedures were experimented with.

The most suitable ways appeared to be:
(1) either a sequential assigning of land use categories to the highest values in the suitability maps, following all the described factors until they reach the requested proportion of landscape within the particular time slice,
(2) using the partially automated methods provided by specific software (like the Hinterland module in IDRISI software, which however leads to more schematic patterns), or
(3) use the benefits of the fully automated procedures integrated in some software packages.

This is essential for that part of modelling where the time-space dynamics of the landscape development are to be simulated. For this purpose several modules in IDRISI of the "Environmental/Simulation Models" dealing with the land changes were designed using especially the cellular automata (such as CA_Markov or the Land Change Modeller, see EASTMAN 2006, 235–260). They are based on the principle of proximity which underlies the dynamics of land change events. In this approach each land use category is assigned the value of a transition probability into another land use class, and the appropriate spatial proportions are calculated for individual time slices (this can be done either automatically or manually). However, with these fully automated procedures we encountered problems with the limited flexibility of the change process (cf. POSKA 2008, 537) especially where it concerns the driving factors. In this case a substantial amount of work would be required to adapt the modules for the particular aspects of archaeological application, such as the manual adjustments of the transition potentials and the spatial extents of subsequent categories. Archaeological evidence finally should serve to palaeo-ecology in modelling as the independent variable which drives the changes in time and shapes the landscape. The problem only lies in its fragmentary character.

Created models/scenarios then are evaluated and validated through "Weights" – sets of codes correlating the probabilistic scenarios to

1) the distance from the core sample or
2) the liability of the predicted landscape categories to be affected by the distance from the core sample (*figure 10*).

Such weights could either be used as one of the criteria in MCE for the creation of suitability maps, or as an independent correlation of completed models. The other validating methods include: statistics (tests of dependence and accordance), historical documents (especially cartographic materials, but with the awareness that post-Medieval and sub-recent landscapes are affected by substantially different economic strategies), and archaeological evidence comprising additional surface prospection, trenching and core sampling.

Conclusion

The results of our preliminary analyses show the future potential of a GIS approach for combining archaeological and pollen data to reconstruct past landscapes with or without human impact. GIS gives insights into the spatial aspects of vegetation/land use composition coming from the pollen data. The benefits of the method presented here lie in the detection of the spatial aspects of the pollen data by correlating them with other features (terrain, soils, geology, archaeology, history etc.). It is apparent that digital modelling of the changing landscape under different past land use systems during different time periods not only offers an intriguing new way to assess the validity of various current archaeological interpretations of land use in prehistory, but also allows us to gain insights into those aspects of the human interaction with landscape that cannot be easily detected from the archaeological record itself.

References Cited

BROSTRÖM, A. – NIELSEN, A. B. – GAILLARD, M. J. – HJELLE, K. – MAZIER, F. – BINNEY, H. – BUNTING, J. – FYFE, R. – MELTSOV, V. – POSKA, A. – RÄSÄNEN, S. – SOEPBOER, W. – VON STEDINGK, H. – SUUTARI, H. – SUGITA, S. 2008: Pollen productivity estimates of key European plant taxa for quantitative reconstruction of past vegetation: a review, *Vegetation History and Archaeobotany* 17, 461–478.

BUNTING, J. – MIDDLETON, R. 2005: Modelling pollen dispersal and deposition using HUMPOL software, including simulating windroses and irregular lakes, *Review of Palaeobotany and Palynology* 134, 185– 196.

BUNTING, M.J. – MIDDLETON, R. 2009: Equifinality and uncertainty in the interpretation of pollen data: the Multiple Scenario Approach to reconstruction of past vegetation mosaic, *The Holocene* 19, 799 – 803.

BUNTING, M.J. – TWIDDLE, C.L. – MIDDLETON, R. 2008: Using models of pollen dispersal and deposition in hilly landscapes: Some possible approaches, *Palaeogeography, Palaeoclimatology, Palaeoecology* 259, 77–91.

CASELDINE, C. – FYFE, R. – HJELLE, K. 2008: Pollen modelling, palaeoecology and archaeology: virtualisation and/ or visualisation of the past?, *Vegetation History and Archaeobotany* 17, 543–549.

CHYTRÁČEK, M. – ŠMEJDA, L. 2005: Opevněný areál na Vladaři a jeho zázemí. K poznání sídelních struktur doby bronzové a železné na horním toku Střely v západních Čechách. (The fortified area at Vladař and its hinterland. Towards an understanding of the settlement structures of the Bronze and Iron Ages in West Bohemia), *Archeologické Rozhledy* 57, 3–56.

DALLA BONNA, L. 1994: Archaeological Predictive Modelling in Ontario´s Forests, http://modelling.pictographics.com/, (accessed March 14, 2010).

EASTMAN, J. R. 2006: *IDRISI Andes. Guide to GIS and Image Processing.* Worcester, MA.

DANIELISOVÁ, A. 2008: Économie et environnement: Habitats de La Tène finale (IIe–Ier s. avant notre ère) en Bohême et Moravie. In : Bertrand, I. – Duval, A. – Gomez de Soto, J. – Maguer, P. (eds.) : *Habitats et paysages ruraux en Gaule et regards sur d´autres régions du monde celtique. Actes du XXXIe colloque international de l´Association Française pour l´Étude de l´Âge du Fer 17–20 mai 2007*, Chauvigny, 299–319.

DANIELISOVÁ, A. 2010: *Oppidum České Lhotice v kontextu svého sídleního zázemí*, (Oppidum České Lhotice and its hinterland), Prague – Pardubice.

DRESLEROVÁ, D. 2008: Ekonomický potenciál regionu Říčanska z hlediska pravěkého hutnictví. In: Venclová, N. et al.: *Hutnický region Říčansko*, Prague, 266–280.

FINDLOW, F. J. – ERICSON, J. E. (eds.) 1980: *Catchment Analysis. Essays on Prehistoric Resource Space,* Los Angeles.

FLANNERY, K. V. 1976: The Village and its Catchment Area. In: Flannery, K.V. (ed.): *The Early Mesoamerican Village,* San Diego – New York – London, 91–103.

FYFE, R. 2006: GIS and the application of a model of pollen deposition and dispersal: a new approach to testing landscape hypotheses using the POLLANDCAL models, *Journal of Archaeological Science* 33, 483–493.

GAFFNEY, V. – VAN LEUSEN, M. 1996: Extending GIS Methods for Regional Archaeology: the Wroxeter Hinterland Project, *Analecta Praehistorica Leidensia* 28, 297–305.

GAILLARD, M.-J. – SUGITA, S. – BUNTING, J. – MIDDLETON, R. – BROSTRÖM, A. – CASELDINE, C. – GIESECKE, T. – HELLMAN, S.E.V. – HICKS, S. – HJELLE, K. – LANGDON, C. – NIELSEN, A.-B. – POSKA, A. –VON STEDINGK, H. – VESKI, S. ETC. 2008: The use of modelling and simulation approach in reconstructing past landscapes from fossil pollen data: a review and results from the POLLANDCAL network, *Vegetation History and Archaeobotany* 17, 419–443.

GARCIA, A. 2008: Predictive Models and the Evolution of Tree Vegetation during the Final Pleistocene-Holocene Transition. A Case Study from the Asón River Valley (Cantabria, Spain). In: Posluschny, A. – Lambers, K. –

Herzog, I. (eds.): *Layers of Perception, Proceedings of the 35ᵗʰ International Conference on Computer Applications and Quantitative Methods in Archaeology (CAA), Berlin, Germany, April 2-6, 2007*, Kolloquien zur Vor- und Frühgeschichte, Vol. 10, Bonn, 392–398.

GAUDIN, L. – MARQUERIE, D. – LANOS, P. 2008: Correlation between spatial distributions of pollen data, archaeological records and physical parameters from northwestern France: a GIS and numerical analysis approach, *Vegetation History and Archaeobotany* 17, 585–595.

GEAREY, B.R. – CHAPMAN, H.P. 2006: "Digital gardening". An approach to simulating elements of palaeovegetation and some implications for the interpretation of prehistoric sites and landscapes. In: Evans, T. L. – Daly, P. (eds.): *Digital Archaeology, bridging method and theory*, London – New York.

GRANT, E. (ed.) 1986: *Central Places, Archaeology and History*, Sheffield.

HAGGET, P. – CLIFF, A.D. – FREY, A. 1977: *Locational Analysis in Human Geography I. II. Locational Models*, London.

HIGGS, E. S. – VITA-FINZI, C. 1972: Prehistoric Economies: a Territorial Approach. In: Higgs, E. S. (ed.): *Papers in Economic Prehistory. Studies by Members and Associates of the British Academy Major Research Project in the Early History of Agriculture*, Cambridge, 27–36.

HLÁSNY, T. 2007: *Geografické informačné systémy, priestorové analýzy*, Banska Bystrica.

KAMERMANS, H. – VAN LEUSEN, M. – VERHAGEN, P. (eds.) 2009: *Archaeological Prediction and Risk Management. Alternatives to Current Practice*, Archaeological studies Leiden University 17, Leiden.

KUNA, M. 2006: Burial mounds in the landscape. In: Šmejda, L. (ed.): *Archaeology of the burial mounds*, Plzeň, 83–97.

KUNA, M. 2008: Analýza polohy pravěkých mohylových pohřebišť pomocí geografických informačních systémů, (An analysis of prehistoric tumulus cemeteries by means of geographic information systems). In: Macháček, J. (ed.): *Počítačová podpora v archeologii 2*, Brno, 79–92.

MEHRER, M. W. – WESTCOTT, K. L. (eds.) 2006: *GIS and Archaeological Site Location Modelling*. Boca Raton – London – New York.

MIDDLETON, R. – BUNTING, J. 2004: Mosaic v1.1: landscape scenario creation software for simulation of pollen dispersal and deposition, *Review of Palaeobotany and Palynology* 132, 61– 66.

NEUSTUPNÝ, E. 2007: *Metoda archeologie*, Plzeň.

NIELSEN, A. B. 2004: Modelling pollen sedimentation in Danish lakes at c. AD 1800: an attempt to validate the POLLSCAPE model, *Journal of Biogeography 31*, 1693–1709.

NIELSEN, A.B. – ODGAARD, B.V. 2005: Reconstructing land cover from pollen assemblages from small lakes in Denmark, *Review of Palaeobotany and Palynology* 133, 1–21.

POKORNÝ, P. – SÁDLO, J. – KAPLAN, M. – MIKOLÁŠKOVÁ, K. – VESELÝ, J. 2005: Paleoenvironmentální výzkum na Vladaři, (Palaeoenvironmental investigations at the hillfort Vladař, Czech Republic), *Archeologické Rozhledy* 57, 57–99.

POKORNÝ, P. – BOENKE, N. – CHYTRÁČEK, M. – NOVÁKOVÁ, K. – SÁDLO, J. – VESELÝ, J. – KUNEŠ, P. – JANKOVSKÁ, V. 2006: Insight into the environment of a pre-Roman Iron Age hillfort at Vladař, Czech Republic, using a multiproxy approach, *Vegetation History and Archaeobotany* 15, 419–433.

POSKA, A. – SEPP, E. – VESKI, S. – KOPPEL, K. 2008: Using quantitative pollen-based land-cover estimations and a spatial CA_Markov model to reconstruct the development of cultural landscape at Roûge, South Estonia, *Vegetation History and Archaeobotany* 17, 527–541.

STANČIČ, Z. – KVAMME, K. L. 1999: Settlement Pattern Modelling through Boolean Overlays of Social and Environmental Variables. In: Barceló – Briz – Assumció (eds.): *New Techniques for Old Times – CAA 98 – Computer Applications and Quantitative Methods in Archaeology. Proceedings of the 26ᵗʰ Conference, Barcelona, March 1998*, BAR International Series 757, Oxford, 231–237.

STEPONAITIS, V. P. 1981: Settlement Hierarchies and Political Complexity in Nonmarket Societies: The Formative Period of the Valley of Mexico, *American Anthropologist, New Series*, Vol. 83, Nº 2, 320–363.

STOBBE, A. 2008: Palynological and Archaeological Data - a Comparative Approach. In: Posluschny, A. – Lambers, K. – Herzog, I. (eds.): *Layers of Perception, Proceedings of the 35ᵗʰ International Conference on Computer Applications and Quantitative Methods in Archaeology (CAA), Berlin, Germany, April 2-6, 2007*, Kolloquien zur Vor- und Frühgeschichte, Vol. 10, Bonn, (on CD).

SUGITA, S. 2007: POLLSCAPE model. In: Elias, S. A. (ed.): *Encyclopedia of quaternary science*. London.

SUGITA, S. 2007a: Theory of quantitative reconstruction of vegetation I: pollen from large sites REVEALS regional vegetation composition, *The Holocene* 17, 229–241.

SUGITA, S. 2007b: Theory of quantitative reconstruction of vegetation II: all you need is LOVE, *The Holocene* 17, 243–257.

SUGITA, S. – GAILLARD, M.-J. – HELLMAN, S. – BROSTRÖM, A. 2008: Model-Based Reconstruction of Vegetation and Landscape Using Fossil Pollen. In: Posluschny, A. – Lambers, K. – Herzog, I. (eds.): *Layers of Perception, Proceedings of the 35th International Conference on Computer Applications and Quantitative Methods in Archaeology (CAA), Berlin, Germany, April 2-6, 2007*, Kolloquien zur Vor- und Frühgeschichte, Vol. 10, Bonn, 385–391.

UCKO, P.J. – TRINGHAM, R. – DIMBLEBY, G.W. (eds.) 1972: *Man, Settlement and Urbanism*. Gloucester.

VAN LEUSEN, M. 2002: *Pattern to Process. Methodological Investigations into the formation and interpretation of spatial patterns in archaeological landscapes*, Groningen.

VERHAGEN, P. 2007: *Case studies in archaeological predictive modelling*, Archaeological studies Leiden University 14.

Alžběta Danielisová
Institute of Archaeology CAS, Prague, v.v.i.
Letenská 4,
118 01 – Prague 1
Czech Republic
danielisova@arup.cas.cz

Petr Pokorný
Institute of Archaeology CAS, Prague, v.v.i.
Letenská 4,
118 01 – Prague 1
Czech Republic
and
Center for Theoretical Study,
Charles University in Prague and the CAS
110 00 – Prague 1
Czech Republic
pokorny@arup.cas.cz

P. Verhagen, A. G. Posluschny, A. Danielisová (eds.)
Proceedings EAA 2009: Go Your Own Least Cost Path, Riva del Garda

Following Roman Waterways from a Computer Screen.
GIS-based Approaches to the Analysis of Barcino's Aqueducts

Hèctor A. Orengo, Carme Miró i Alaix

Abstract

From the 1950's until today the Roman colony of Barcino (modern Barcelona) has been believed to posses two aqueducts. One was transporting water from the Montcada mountains and the other one from the Collserola range. In this article, GIS-based least-cost route analysis (LCR) in combination with more traditional archaeological techniques is applied to analyse these aqueduct's routes. The results obtained suggest Barcino had only one aqueduct: the one carrying water from Montcada. The aqueduct was divided in two channels before entering the city, thus giving origin to the theories suggesting the existence of two aqueducts. LCR analysis has also been useful in determining the medieval transformation of this aqueduct into the Rec Comtal water channel.

Introduction

Water supply was a key function of Roman public services, it covered numerous public and private needs in Roman cities. Roman engineers were particularly efficient at designing and constructing water collecting, transport, storage and distribution systems which supplied public and private baths, fountains, gardens and pools, dwellings and industries. Roman cities consumed significantly more water per person than modern ones, at least judging by the example of Imperial Rome (FORBES 1955, HODGE 2000, 47–49). It is not clichéd to state that Roman culture was intimately related to water use (ORENGO ET AL. IN PRESS). Not in vain, PLINY THE ELDER (Nat. XXXI 2.4) evokes the power of water to create cities. Therefore, the choice of an adequate source of water was an important one. Different types of water were selected according to their intended use, that being medicinal, potable, sanitary, industrial or recreational. Some of the most noteworthy examples in this sense are the construction of the Aqua Alsietina, an aqueduct directed at supplying the Naumachia of Augustus, an artificial lake in the Trastevere in which recreational naval battles would be performed or the Aqua Virgo, constructed to supply the thermae of Agrippa in Campo Marzio (STACCIOLI 2002, 56–65). Transporting water from far away sources could easily pay off the large effort required to achieve this, when a constant and adequate supply was guaranteed and the water was pure enough. Roman authors, in fact, attached much importance to water qualities (VITRUVIUS 8, 4, 1–2; FRONTINUS 11, 1–2). Water quality could save maintenance costs preventing the settling of sinter on the channel walls or silt at the bottom. In this sense, Roman engineers were, to a certain degree, more concerned about the quality and quantity of water supplied

Figure 1. Aqueduct entrances into the city.

by a certain source than the distance the water had to be transported (HODGE 2000, 49; MALISSARD 2001, 151-153). Numerous examples can be provided which show the enormous distances covered by aqueducts to obtain good quality water in exchange (HODGE 2000, 65).

Barcino's aqueducts

This work intends to present the first results of a project dedicated to the study of water sources, management, distribution, use and disposal in the Roman colony of Barcino (modern Barcelona). The project was started in 2009 by the Catalan Institute of Classical Archaeology (ICAC) and the Museum of the History of Barcelona (MUHBA) (MIRÓ – ORENGO 2010). The first stage of the project consisted in the analysis of Barcino's Roman aqueducts. Since the 1960's it is considered that this city was supplied with water from different springs by means of two aqueducts. This belief came from the discovery of two aqueduct channels in the tower of one of Barcino's Roman gates *(figure 1)*. This tower was the entrance for the water channels to the city for its urban distribution. Later, excavations carried

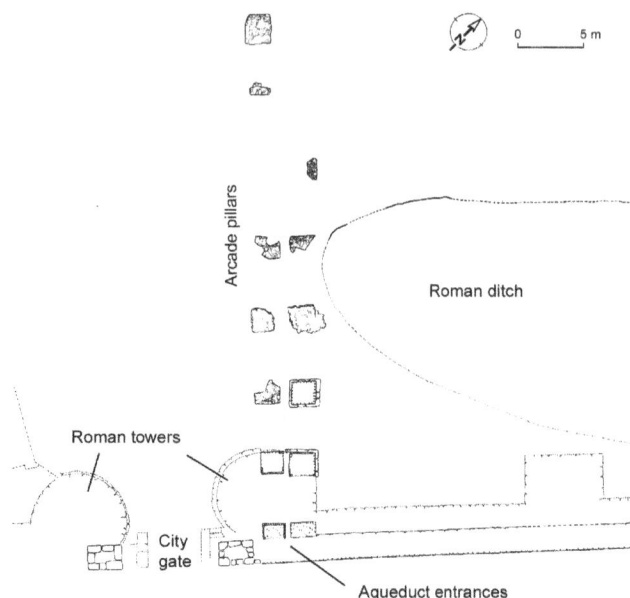

Figure 2. Arcade pillar bases archaeologically documented.

out next to this tower, unearthed a series of pillars corresponding to the two arcades bearing the channels found inside the tower (*figure 2*). These findings were interpreted as being part of two aqueducts carrying water to the city from different sources which joined at this point to enter the city through the same entrance.

A short history of the research carried out about them, referred as the Montcada and the Collserola aqueducts from this point onwards, is presented here.

The Montcada aqueduct
Evidence of this aqueduct can be found in written documents dating back to the Xth century. The discovery in 1987 of a preserved arcade of five contiguous arches with the aqueduct channel still intact on top of them, some 160 m away from the Roman city gate contributes to the written evidence concerning the form and route of this aqueduct inside Barcelona's medieval quarter. The recent discovery of a 90 m subterranean stretch of aqueduct at 6.7 km north of the city (GINER 2006) corroborates the idea, already suggested by the medieval documents, that this aqueduct supplied water from the springs located in the Montcada mountains, some 9 km north from the city. Most of the aqueduct was a subterranean conduit which, as it approached the city was elevated by means of arcades. This conduit route has been generally acknowledged to coincide with that of Rec Comtal, a Xth century channel used to supply hydraulic energy for numerous mills and water to irrigate several areas of Barcelona's plain. Early medieval documents and archaeological evidence seem to support this theory. The route of Rec Comtal, unlike that of Montcada aqueduct's, deviated before reaching the Roman city cen-

tre in order to provide water to the industrial areas of the medieval city.

The Collserola aqueduct
The analysis of XVIIth and XVIIIth century documents and toponymic evidence lead MAYER AND RODÀ (1977) to propose that the Collserola Range springs were the origin of this second aqueduct. They also proposed a route for this aqueduct which traversed Barcelona's plain in a straight line from Collserola to the entrance of the aqueducts in Barcino equivalent to that of the XIVth century pressurized piped conduit which supplied the fountains of medieval and modern Barcelona (XIVth–XVIIIth centuries).

Sources and Methods

The cartographic database
In order to study the characteristic features of Barcino's aqueducts, a specific GIS-based cartographic dataset had to be constructed. This posed a number of problems that are not usually acknowledged in GIS-based landscape studies. Firstly, and most importantly, Barcelona's territory has undergone dramatic change since the Roman period (PALET 1997; PALET ET AL. 2009). Such landscape changes, which have mostly occurred during the second half of the XIXth and the XXth century, have had irreversible effects on the territory's topography, rendering modern digital terrain models (DTMs) useless. In order to somewhat reduce the effects of modern construction work in the area, a series of XIXth century and early XXth century topographic maps were selected and georeferenced using a regressive cartographic database. That is, modern maps were employed to obtain Ground Control Points (GCPs) which in turn could be used to georeference older ones from which new GCPs could be obtained. This process permitted the creation of a database with more than 300 of no longer available GCPs which in turn allowed georeferencing the oldest cartographic elements. The combination of the different georeferenced old topographic maps permitted a reading of the area without the most evident modern landscape modifications and thus facilitated the development of a hypothetical topographic map of the area in pre-industrial times.

The geographic database also included a series of 1:2.000 aerial photographs made in 1947. These were georeferenced and orthorectified using GCPs obtained from the georeferenced cartographic database.

Reconstruction of the Rec Comtal route
The analysis of old cartography and old aerial photographs was employed to locate ancient traces of the Rec Comtal route. By combining the morphological information present in georeferenced ancient maps and orthophotographs, the Rec Comtal route was reconstructed (*figure 3*) to a high degree of precision (a maximum ground error of 1.5 m).

Written and archaeological evidence
The first step in the study of Barcino's Roman aqueducts

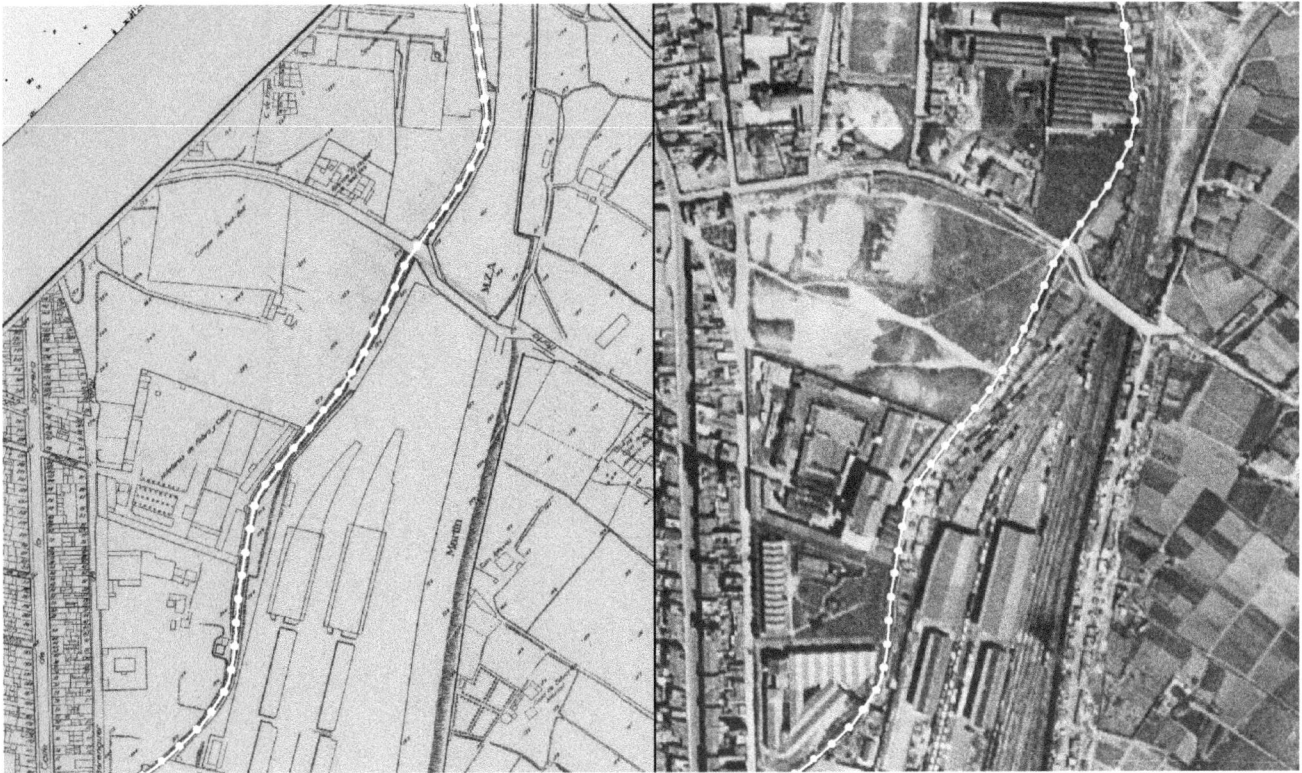

Figure 3. Cartographic and photographic reconstruction of the Rec Comtal route.

was the positioning of the different types of evidence which can offer any geographically located information on the ancient trace of the aqueducts. Medieval written evidence which related to the location of the aqueducts was also introduced in the GIS. A total number of 25 documents corresponding to dates between the Xth and the XIXth century were introduced into a database which contained their geographical location, their documentary reference and the quoted text. An epigraphic document in Latin found in Camí de Jesús which related to the city's water management was also introduced. Another layer was constituted by the archaeologically documented remains of the aqueducts. Their plans were digitised, georeferenced and vectorised.

Least Cost Route Analysis
LCR has been employed in the analysis of Roman aqueduct routes before (BAENA ET AL. 1998; ROLDÁN ET AL. 1999, LAGÓSTENA – ZULETA 2009, 165-166). Unfortunately, there is little explanation in these works about the methodology followed or the algorithm employed. This might be caused by the fact that Least-Cost Route (LCR) analysis alone cannot be employed to model the trace of a water channel. Due to the specific characteristics of aqueducts which combine a constructed trace and a water flow, they do not obey cultural, topographic or hydrologic conditionings alone but a combination of them all. None the less, aqueducts are landscape structures, they adapt to the territory's topography to a certain extent (HODGE 2000, 54–55) and this essential topographic adaptation makes LCR analysis an especially adequate tool to analyse them.

Having said that, several characteristics of aqueducts have to be taken into account when modelling their route:
- They only flow in one direction so anisotropic models are to be preferred.
- They follow a downhill route.
- Their gradient is constant.
- Excessive downward slope is not supported by unpressurized conduits.
- They can also incorporate engineering works such as cascades, tunnels, siphons or arcades which allow them, to a certain degree, to overcome topographic restraints.
- They also show an interest in monumentality which can motivate the use of arcades when not topographically necessary.

The development of LCRs based on cost surfaces has been acknowledged as a useful methodological approach in the archaeological analysis of movement. However, as has already been pointed out, the use of LCR alone cannot produce valid results but it should be directed towards an exploratory analysis (Fiz and Orengo 2008). In this sense, the results of the cartographic and photographic analyses of the Rec Comtal and the locations suggested by the different documents referring to the aqueduct's traces will be essential in modelling the most appropriate route. The model will be tried and refined using the archaeological evidence known for the Montcada aqueduct. This model will then be applied to the reconstruction of the second aqueduct, the one bringing waters from the Collserola Range.

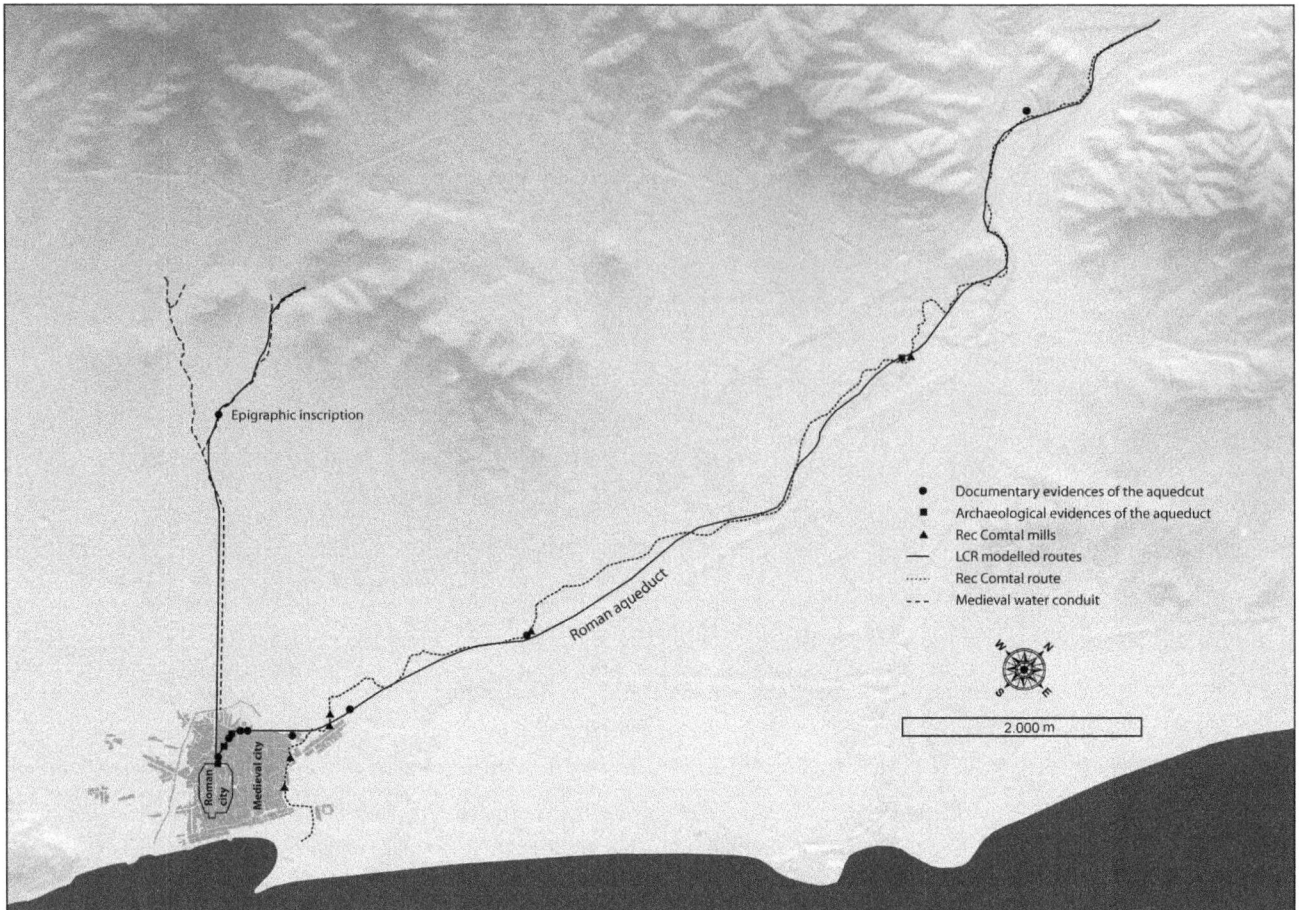

Figure 4. Reconstruction of the Roman aqueduct, the Rec Comtal and Medieval conduit routes.

To develop a cost surface which could effectively reflect the friction parameters affecting the route of the aqueduct, the GRASS GIS module *r.walk* was chosen (FONTANARI 2002). This anisotropic function incorporates the formula published by AITKEN (1977) and LANGMUIR (1984) based on Naismith's rule for walking times:

T= [(a)*(ΔS)] + [(b)*(ΔH uphill)] + [(c)*(ΔH moderate downhill)] + [(d)*(ΔH steep downhill)]

Where:
T is time of movement in seconds, ΔS is the distance covered in meters and ΔH is the altitude difference in meters. The default parameters, developed originally to calculate walking times, were adapted to define the factors involved in the setting of a Roman aqueduct thus favouring moderate downhill and strongly discouraging both uphill and steep downhill movements:
a (cost of movement): 0.5
b (cost of movement uphill): 200
c (cost of movement moderate downhill): 0.1
d (cost of movement steep downhill): -200
The slope value threshold is -0.017 (corresponding to tan (-0.974°)). Values exceeding this threshold will be regarded as steep downhill and they will therefore incur in increased cost values. As HERZOG has pointed out (2010), the *r.walk* function can be inadequate when calculating walking costs due to the harsh cost increase marked by the slope threshold. In this case study, the threshold is equal to the maximum evidenced slope of an unpressurised Roman aqueduct, corresponding to a slope of 17 m/km or 0.974°. Beyond this value Roman engineers would employ techniques such as cascades of arcades which will enormously increase the aqueduct's cost. In this sense, the *r.walk* function inadequacies for calculating walking times can be overcome when applied to the analysis of water channels. The *r.walk* module also permits to employ the knight's move in the cost surface generation which results in a more accurate analysis.

Once generated the least cost surface, the aqueduct route was determined by the module *r.drain* which would trace a water flow from the origin point trough the *r.walk* generated cost surface until the aqueduct entrances into Barcino. The results of this analysis will be useful in gaining a better knowledge of the conditions affecting the design and construction of Barcino's Roman aqueducts as well as to analyse their routes.

Results

The Montcada aqueduct

The proposed LCR for the Roman aqueduct of Montcada coincides with the path followed by Rec Comtal as evidenced by cartographic and photographic interpretation. It is also coincident with the archaeological and documentary evidence of the Roman aqueduct. Two main differences have been encountered between the routes followed by the Rec Comtal and the Roman aqueduct (*figure 4*). Firstly, Rec Comtal diverts before entering the Roman city. Secondly, the trace of Rec Comtal is clearly more sinuous than that of the LCR modelled Roman aqueduct. It shows various diversions which at first follow the contours and later break them to get the maximum slope until it reunites with the ancient aqueduct trace. Ancient map analysis and documentary evidence show that these deviations coincided with the location of medieval and modern mills. After detailed microtopographical analysis it becomes obvious that these deviations' purpose was to keep the water flow level only to later make it descend abruptly and thus take advantage of the increase in water speed. Mills were constructed at the points of highest water speed (*figure 5*).

The Roman aqueduct was employed in the Middle Ages as a topographical guide in the construction of the Rec Comtal open channel. This use has also been documented in the construction of Mina de l'Arquebisbe, a water conduction which also followed the traces of one of Tarraco's Roman aqueducts (LÓPEZ 2008, 368).

The total length of the aqueduct would be 11.3 km covering a total height difference of only 18.12 m. The water flow inclination would be 1.6 m/km, a rather conservative proportion for a Roman aqueduct according to the standards recorded in the archaeological bibliography (HODGE 2000, 50–51). There was indeed some divergence amongst Roman authors: VITRUVIUS (VII 6.1) specified a 5 m/km slope, whereas PLINY (Nat. XXXI 57), closer to the actual archaeological evidence, stated that the ideal slope had to be 0.2 m/km.

The Collserola aqueduct

Concerning the Collserola aqueduct, the proposed LCR shows a remarkable similarity with the traces of the medieval conduit bringing water from the Collserola springs. However, no archaeological trace of its existence in Roman times has been found. XVIIth and XVIIIth century documentary evidence relates to the medieval water conduits only. The inscription found at Camí de Jesús can also be linked to this medieval conduit. Epigraphic analysis conducted by D. Gorostidi indicates a XVIth-XVIIth century origin for this document. It may be related to a modern monumentalisation of the medieval conduit.

The LCR proposed route for this conduct was 6.4 km long with an average slope of 38.45 m/km. This slope (*figure 6*) is significantly higher than any other known Roman aqueduct or inverted siphon system. This is so, even if only

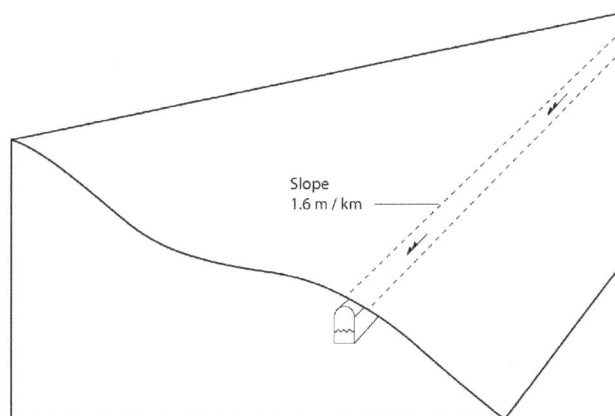

Roman aqueduct

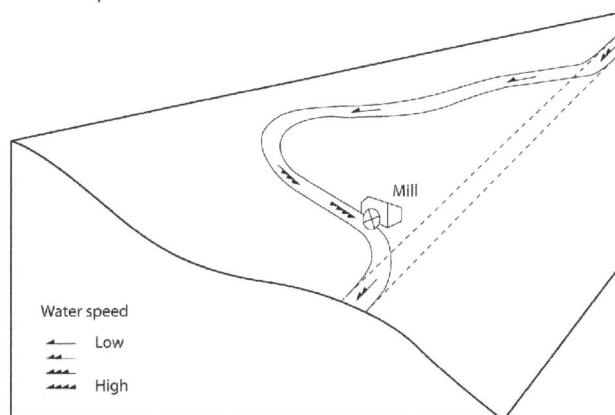

Rec Comtal

Figure 5. Comparison between the Roman Montcada aqueduct and Rec Comtal.

the last part of its route, outside Collserola range, is considered. In this case the distance would be of 2.98 km with a gradient of 17.87 m/km.

Conclusions

Historical conclusions

Considering all the data provided by the different sources, the Roman origin of the Montcada aqueduct becomes evident, whereas the Collserola aqueduct does not meet Roman engineering standards and does not show any evidence of a pre-medieval origin. It is also interesting to compare the varying water discharge levels of the different water sources. The Montcada water mine had, according to a technical enquiry conducted in 1895, a minimum discharge of 38804 m³ per day (MARTÍN 2007, 313) while the Collserola water mines discharged around 300 m³ per day (CALL 1878, 124). This is clearly an insufficient amount to justify the construction of a water conduit, particularly if the amount of water supplied by the Montcada sources is taken into account.

Furthermore, the quality of water that these channels transport should also be taken into account. The preserved stretches of channel from the Montcada aqueduct do not show any evidence of sinter deposits within them. On the

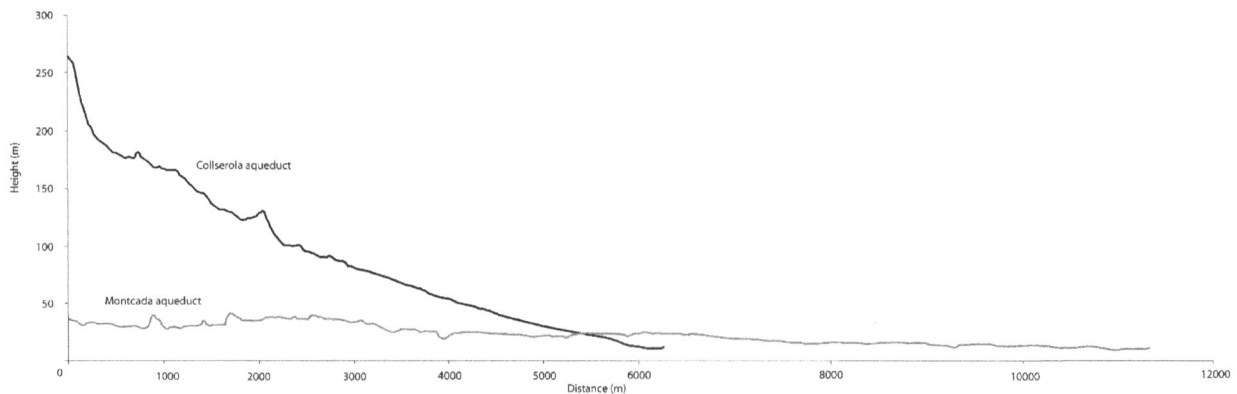

Figure 6. Comparison between the Collseorla and Montacada aqueduct profiles.

contrary, medieval documents recording water transport from the Collserola range springs made evident the need for continuous cleansing of sinter deposits in the water conduit (SCHWARTZ – CARRERAS CANDI 1892, 385; VOLTES 1967, 28, 38). In this respect, it is worth mentioning that the two channels entering Barcino presented no traces of sinter.

All this evidence leads us to assume Barcino had only one aqueduct, corresponding to the Montcada aqueduct, which considering the colony size was more than enough to cover its needs. The existence of two aqueduct entrances to the city must be related to a split of the Montcada aqueduct before entering the city. The water transported by these two channels was probably destined to cover unrelated functions within the city.

The Collserola conduit needs to be considered as medieval in origin. At the Xth century the Roman aqueduct has fallen into disuse and the Rec Comtal water was destined to agricultural and industrial functions and therefore many wells had to be excavated throughout the city to replace the water brought in by the Roman aqueduct. Some factors such as population growth or processes of desiccation and salinization of the wells probably forced medieval authorities to construct this new conduit in order to supply the medieval city towards the second half of the XIVth century.

Technical conclusions

The use of GIS and related topographic analysis has been essential in order to analyse the route of the aqueducts and its relationship to the landscape topographic settings. In the case of the Montcada aqueduct these analyses allowed the comparison between the Roman aqueduct and Rec Comtal evidencing the relationship between the Rec Comtal deviations and the new function of the medieval channel. They also provided information which allowed discarding the Collserola range as the origin of a second Roman aqueduct, as it has been believed up until now.

It is also evidenced that LCR analysis should be employed as an exploratory rather than an explanatory tool. Only by combining LCR with archaeological and historical data LCR can provide useful hints about the route of

topographically related structures in the landscape such as roads or aqueducts and the way they were conceived and constructed.

References cited

AITKEN, R. 1977. *Wilderness areas in Scotland*. Unpublished Ph.D. thesis. University of Aberdeen.

BAENA, J. – BLASCO, C. – ROLDÁN, L. – ALMONACID, C. – BERMÚDEZ, J. – CARRO, I. – RIO, A. – ESPIAGO, J. 1998. Applications of GIS to the archaeology of Roman Hispania. In: Peterson, J. (ed.) *The use of Geographic Information Systems in the study of ancient landscapes and features related to ancient land use*. European Commission, COST ACTION G2, Paysages antiques et structures rurales. Directorate-General. Science, Research and Development: 1–20.

CALL I FRANQUEZA, D. 1878. *Colección de los artículos que con el epígrafe "Mejoras de Barcelona" publicó en el Diario de Barcelona*. Barcelona, Suc. de Ramírez y Cia.

FIZ, I. – ORENGO, H.A. 2008. Simulating communication routes in Mediterranean alluvial plains. In: Posluschny, A. – Lambers, K. – Herzog, I. (eds.) *Layers of Perception. Proceedings of the 35th International Conference on Computer Applications and Quantitative Methods in Archaeology (CAA), Berlin, Germany, April 2–6, 2007*, Kolloquien zur Vor- und Frühgeschichte, vol. 10. Bonn, Habelt: 316–321.

FONTANARI, S. 2002. *Sviluppo di metodologie GIS per la determinazione dell'accessibilita territoriale come supporto alle decisioni nella gestione ambientale*. Unpublished M.Sc. dissertation. University of Trento.

FORBES, R.J. 1955. *Studies in ancient technology*. Volume 1. Leiden, E.J. Brill.

GINER, D. 2006. *Memòria de la intervenció arqueològica preventiva al C/. Coronel Monasterio 6 – 16 (Barcelona,* el Barcelonès). Març - agost de 2004. Unpublished report. Centre de Documentació, MUHBA.

HERZOG, I. 2010. Theory and Practice of Cost Functions. In: Contreras, F – Melero, F. J. (eds.) *Fusion of Cultures. Proceedings of the 38th Conference on Computer Applications and Quantitative Methods in Archaeology. Granada, Spain, April 2010.*

HODGE, A.T. 2000. I.5. Aqueducts. In: Wikander, O. (ed.) *Handbook of ancient Water Technology.* Leiden, Boston, Köln, Brill: 39–65.

LAGÓSTENA, L.G. – ZULETA, F. DE B. 2009. Gades y su acueducto: una revisión. In: Lagóstena, L.G. – Zuleta, F. de B. (coords.) *La captación, los usos y la administración del agua en Baetica: Estudios sobre el abastecimiento hídrico en comunidades cívicas del Conventus Gaditanus.* Cádiz, Servicio de Publicaciones de la Universidad de Cádiz: 115–170.

LANGMUIR, E. 1984. *Mountaincraft and leadership.* The Scottish Sports Council/MLTB. Leicester, Cordee.

LÓPEZ, J. 2008. L'Aqüeducte del Gaià. In: Vergés, J. M. – López, J. (coords.) *Valls i la seva història.* Volum II. Prehistòria i història antiga. Valls, Institut d'Estudis Vallencs.

MALISSARD, A. 2001. *Los romanos y el agua.* Barcelona, Herder.

MARTÍN, J.M. 2007. *Aigua i societat a Barcelona entre les dues exposicions* (1888–1929). Unpublished Ph.D. thesis. Universitat Autònoma de Barcelona.

MAYER, M. – RODÀ, I. 1977. *El abastecimiento de aguas en la Barcelona romana. Reconstrucción de su trazado.* Segovia y la Arqueología romana, actas del Symposium de Arqueología romana (Segovia, 1974): 265–277.

MIRÓ, C. – ORENGO, H.A. 2010. El cicle de l'aigua a Barcino. Una reflexió entorn a les noves dades arqueològiques. *Quaderns d'arqueologia i història de la ciutat de Barcelona,* època II, 6: 108–133.

ORENGO, H. A. – EJARQUE, A. – ALBIACH, R. In press. Water management practices from Iberian to Roman times in la Carència hinterland (Valencia, Spain). In: Trément, F. (ed.), *Colloque ZAL,* Clermont-Ferrand.

PALET, J.M. 1997. *Estudi territorial del Pla de Barcelona.* Estructuració i evolució del territori entre l'època ibero-romana i l'altmedieval. Segles II-I aC – X-XI dC, Estudis i Memòries d'Arqueologia de Barcelona, 1. Barcelona, Ajuntament de Barcelona.

PALET, J. M. – FIZ, I. – ORENGO, H. A. 2009. Centuriació i estructuració de l'ager de la Colònia de Barcino: anàlisi arqueomorfològica i modelació del paisatge. *Quaderns d'arqueologia i història de la ciutat de Barcelona,* època II, 5: 106–123.

STACCIOLI, R.A. 2002. *Acquedotti, fontane e terme di Roma antica.* Roma, Newton & Compton Editori.

SCHWARTZ, F. – CARRERAS CANDI, F. (eds.) 1892. *Manual de Novells Ardits, vulgarment apellat.* Dietari del Antich Consell Barceloní. Volúm primer, comprenent los volúms originals del I al IX. Anys 1390–1446.

ROLDÁN, L. – BAENA, J. – BLASCO, C. – BERMÚDEZ, J. – GARCÍA, E. 1999. SIG y arqueología romana. Restitución del trazado del acueducto de Cádiz. In: Baena, J. – Blasco, C. – Quesada, F. (eds.) *Los S.I.G. y el análisis espacial en arqueología.* Madrid, Ediciones de la Universidad Autónoma de Madrid: 255–272.

VOLTES, P. 1967. *Historia del abastecimiento de agua de Barcelona.* Barcelona, Sociedad General de Aguas de Barcelona.

Hèctor A. Orengo
Landscape Archaeology Research Group - Catalan
Institute of Classical Archaeology (GIAP-ICAC)
Pl. Rovellat s/n
43003, Tarragona, Spain
horengo@icac.net

Carme Miró i Alaix
Museum of the History of Barcelona (MUHBA)
Plaça del Rei, s/n
08002, Barcelona
cmiro@bcn.cat

P. Verhagen, A. G. Posluschny, A. Danielisová (eds.)
Proceedings EAA 2009: Go Your Own Least Cost Path, Riva del Garda

Sherds on the Map.
Intra-site GIS of the Neolithic Site of Bylany (Czech Republic)

Petr Květina, Markéta Končelová

Abstract

The aim of this paper is to point out the capabilities of GIS technology to solve questions of micro-scale formation processes of the archaeological record. Micro-scale spatial analysis is rarely applied in archaeology outside hunter-gatherer studies. This case study is based on data obtained during rescue excavations at the Neolithic site of Bylany (Czech Republic). The excavation method applied here enabled research into the formation processes of archaeological materials at the scale of individual pits. The obtained data were processed and analyzed in ArcGIS 9.3 and its extensions Spatial Analyst and 3D Analyst. The result consisted of a spatial model of the particular pit including its fill layers and individual artefacts. The model leads to an interpretation of the depositional history of the pit. This history apparently reflects a series of events that are mostly the result of intentional human activity.

Starting Points

The idea to study formation processes of archaeological material at the micro-scale of the individual pits was formulated in 2004 during the rescue excavation of the Bylany site (*figure 1*). The area of the rescue excavation was adjacent to the original section B of the Bylany 1 area and captured the edge of a settlement area that becomes more dispersed in the direction of an unnamed waterway. The question addressed is related to the way of pit filling: is it possible to determine whether the given feature was intentionally filled after the end of its primary functioning or whether the fill was the result of subsequent natural processes? A special method was applied – it consisted in segment excavation and the exact registration of archaeological finds. The software package ArcGIS 9.3 was used to create a 3D feature model and to project the finds' positions, which in turn allowed for analysis and subsequent interpretation.

Figure 1. *Plan of excavated areas A, B and F showing the assumed total space of the Neolithic settlement. For settlement chronology see* http://www.bylany.com/images/Bylany%20chronology.jpg.

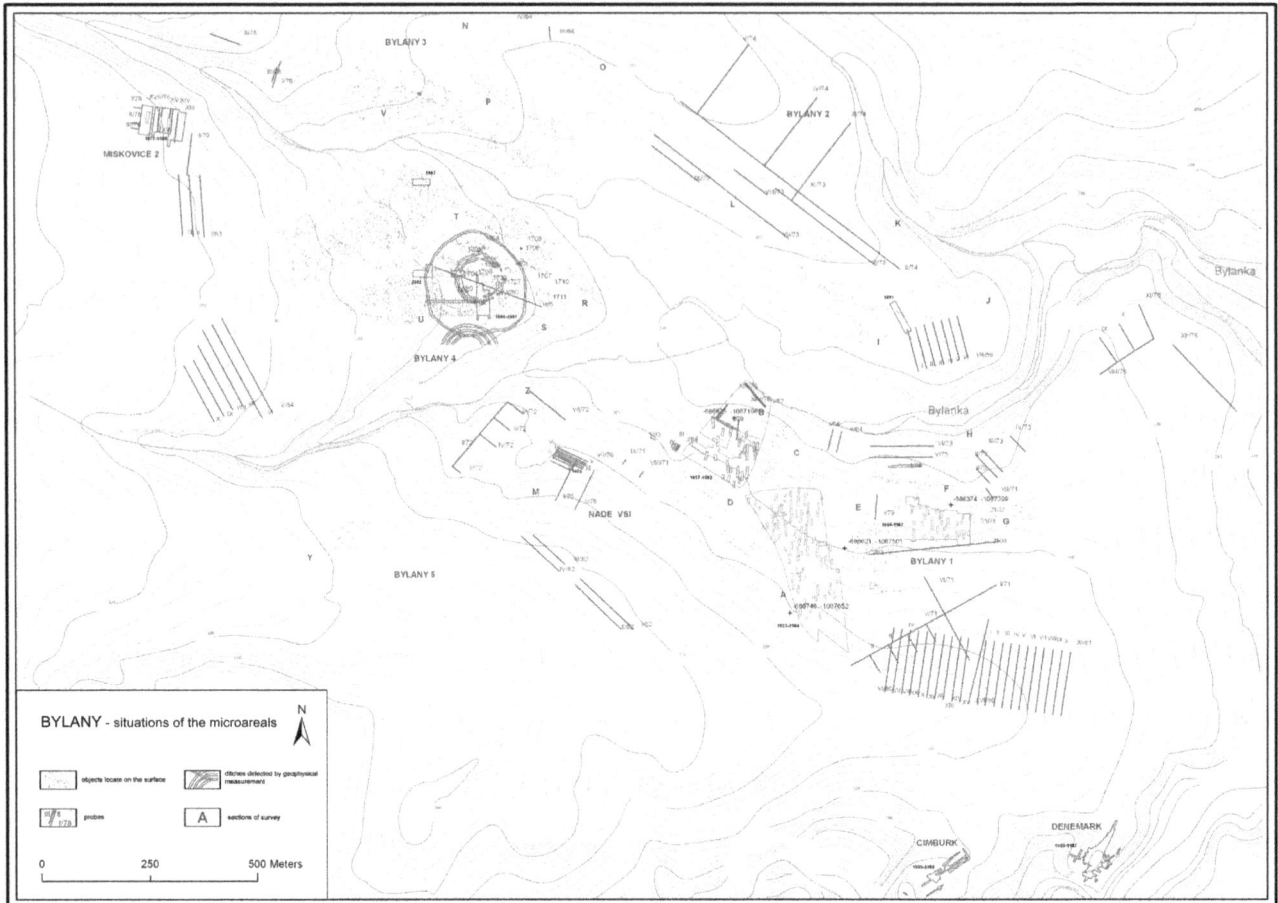

Figure 2. Plan of the micro-areas at the Bylany site.

Concise history of the Bylany site (Czech Republic)

The excavation at Bylany was unique in its time because of the large-scale excavation method used and the application of formalized descriptions of archaeological data suitable for automated processing. The site awakened professional interest in the research of settlement areas of the first farmers in Central Europe (Linear Pottery culture or LBK)[1]. The first excavations at the site are associated with B. Soudský, whose work was continued by I. Pavlů, M. Zápotocká and J. Rulf. The field activities and subsequent processing of the finds have produced numerous studies that have had a significant impact on the excavation methodology utilized at Neolithic sites and the analysis of archaeological material for this and other periods (e.g. SOUDSKÝ 1962; SOUDSKÝ - PAVLŮ 1972; PAVLŮ – RULF – ZÁPOTOCKÁ 1986; PAVLŮ – RULF – ZÁPOTOCKÁ 1995; PAVLŮ 2000). At the same time, they have also modified the interpretation of the society and culture of early farmers in the Czech territory and beyond.

The history of archaeological excavations in Bylany can be divided into four distinct phases: Large-scale excavations were executed between 1953 and 1967; nearly 7 ha were studied and divided into three separate areas labeled A, B and F (*figure 1*). Even though only one-third of the originally planned excavations of the site (Bylany 1) was conducted, the site remains to this day the largest Neolithic settlement continuously studied in Bohemia. The main outcome of this phase of excavations was the establishment of the internal chronology of the settlement. It also proved that the discovered settlement is a non-homogeneous spatiotemporal unit composed of several components.

In the subsequent period (1968–1989) excavations concentrated on the structure of the Neolithic settlement and that of the entire micro-region. The plan specifically included probing the BYLANY1-BYLANY5 micro-sites (*figure 2*), and field excavations of the Kutná Hora 2, Nové Dvory 1 and 2, Hlízov and Miskovice 2 micro-sites.

In the years 1990–1993, excavations concentrated at detecting and understanding the mutual relationships within the spatiotemporally demarcated site (project "Model of the Neolithic site" (PAVLŮ – RULF – ZÁPOTOCKÁ 1995)). The complex of Bylany Late Neolithic rondels (circular earthworks) was excavated as part of this program (MIDGLEY ET AL. 1993).

---

[1] This work was done with support from the research project at the Institute of Archaeology of the Academy of Sciences of the Czech Republic, Prague, entitled: "The archaeological potential of Bohemia: theoretical research, methodology and information science, care for national cultural heritage." Identification code AV0Z80020508.

Since the year 2000 the systematic transformation of the Bylany documentation has progressed; its goal is the publication of a compact set containing a database, illustrations and a GIS map, both on digital media (Květina – Pavlů 2007) and on the internet in a Czech/English version (2009–2010). This phase also included archaeological rescue excavations bordering the original B area, during which the question regarding the formation processes of the archaeological material was addressed.

The Bylany database: what is the best way to publish the extensive amount of archaeological information?

Bylany became internationally known not only for its excavation methods, but at the time especially thanks to a unique approach to processing large assemblages of archaeological finds. Unlike many other large archaeological excavations being conducted in Czechoslovakia in that period, the material gathered at the site was also regularly evaluated, beginning in 1966, by using a formalized description created for these very purposes. Owing to an enormous amount of acquired archaeological material and documentation accompanying these finds, B. Soudský suggested to utilize punch cards to automate the evaluation process (Soudský 1967). In terms of archaeological method, this was one of the first applications of computing devices in Central Europe.

In the 1980s the complete drawing documentation was published (Pavlů – Zápotocká 1983, Pavlů – Zápotocká– Soudský 1985, Pavlů – Zápotocká – Soudský 1987). These „blue" catalogues contain archaeological structures and all of the diagnostic data concerning fragments of pottery and stone artefacts. Additional supplementary Bylany data were published in the thematic series Bylany Varia, where, for example, a summary of eco-data was published (Peške – Rulf – Slavíková 1998). Also published in this series was the first attempt at adding descriptors relating to the formation processes of archaeological material (Last 1998).

Nevertheless, although the status of the release of the Bylany data is exceptional in comparison to similar archaeological research projects, the publication of the data in printed form does not offer good prospects for their further use. The fact that the data still conceal a large amount of uncovered structures is documented by some contemporary thematic works (Květina in print). For these reasons, it was decided to present the Bylany data in digital form, both on a website and on CD with a printed metadata manual (Květina – Pavlů 2007). This publication is composed of:
1. A metadata manual and
2. A disc with a database, illustrations (finds, features) and shapefiles connected to the GIS map.

The disc comprises two levels. A simple interface was de-

signed for the first (basic) level: a scheme containing prepared forms with basic filters that allow users to link the database with the illustrations (in .pdf-format). Primary categories offered include features, houses, pottery, non-pottery artefacts and the possibility to access the tables (in .mdb-format). Each item then contains the possibility of displaying the given context, house or finds on the basis of find numbers along with data on the position at the site, the section and also their characteristic and metric description. The second level - intended for advanced users - enables more progressive data analysis through the creation of relational queries. However, it is necessary to point out that the user in this case will need to become familiarized with the metadata manual. This handbook includes a complete explanation and thesaurus of the database's descriptive codes. The structure of the database itself is composed of 16 basic tables and is completely available in an English version including a manual. Individual database fields, descriptors and separate entities are explained in both written form and by means of numerous illustrations and references to literature. For easier and clearer orientation in the Bylany data, a GIS map of the site is attached in shapefile format; the map can be connected to tables to enable users to create their own spatial queries.

The basic scheme (the primary database level) was adapted for the needs of functioning on the internet and was released at http://www.bylany.com. This internet interface enables a basic search of the attributes and is accompanied by the necessary manual. The advantage that releasing the database system on the Internet has over digital media is the possibility of adding information or correcting any errors potentially occurring with such a volume of data. We believe that this method of presenting data is the optimal solution today.

The database facilitates the analysis of various levels of data such as settlement chronology and artefact function. It can also be used for less common analyses focused on the formative processes of archaeological material. The following article presents a methodical illustration of this type of approach.

Micro-GIS evidence and analysis of settlement refuse

The essential research questions in this case study focus on the issue whether detailed records of the positions of finds in archaeological structures can be used to solve problems relating to the formation processes of archaeological material. The specific question being investigated was formulated as follows: is it possible to determine whether the given feature was intentionally filled after the end of its primary functioning or whether the fill was the result of subsequent natural processes? This is one of the topics that recently received new attention by the debate on the intentional deposition of objects outside of a systematic context, e.g. in the form of "structured" deposition according to J. Chapman (Chapman - Gaydarska 2007).

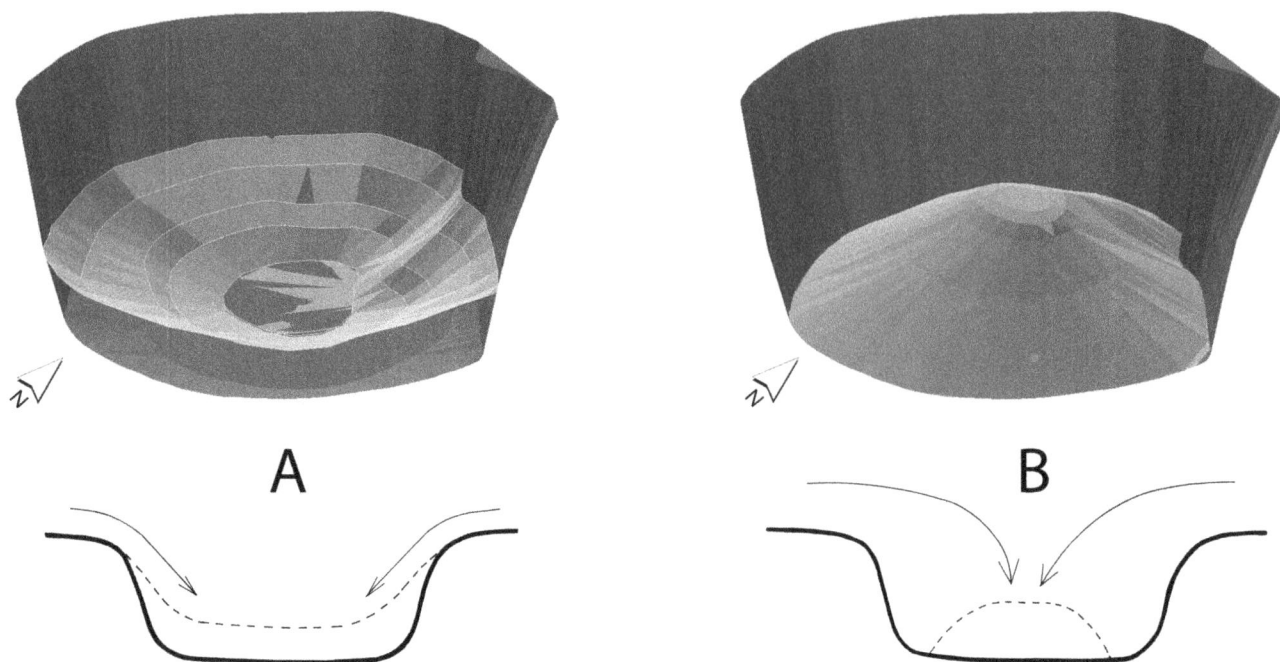

Figure 3. Models of natural (A) and cultural (B) agents causing the filling of the pit.

Two possible hypotheses explaining filling of the pit were formulated at the outset of the research (*figure 3*). They defined the basic processes by which archaeological findings could enter the pit no. 2385 at the end of its primary functioning. The first model explains the origin of a pit fill as an unintentional natural process caused by gravity and the wash-off of material around the pit. These processes occur gradually with smaller and greater fluctuations influenced by climatic conditions at the given time. Diagram A in *figure 3* shows a model for the natural creation of the fill. The artefacts in this case fall or shift along the pit walls, and the resulting fill has a concave shape. The initial sharp angle at which the artefacts fall or wash into the pit gradually dulls as the pit fills. The heavier and larger artefacts typically move down along the sides, causing them to collect in the middle of the pit. The slope of the land on which the pit is situated also plays a large role in the final position of the finds: the parts of the pit angling down the slope therefore contain more finds. The natural filling of the pit ends once the fill reaches the level of the surrounding terrain.

The other possible way of pit filling is by means of cultural and intentional processes, which means the deliberate deposition of objects in the pit. The removal and cleaning of refuse from busy places to zones where the refuse does not interfere is a general cultural phenomenon confirmed by ethno-archaeological excavations (DEAL 1985; DEBOER AND LATHRAP 1979; GRAHAM 1994; HAYDEN – CANNON 1983). Refuse is deposited, for example, at the edge of land parcels, homesteads and settlements, and abandoned features are often used for this purpose. Land depressions and pits are regarded as certain "traps" that attract refuse (WILK – SCHIFFER 1979, 534). If they are present

at a settlement, pits represent the simplest solution for refuse management. Material in this case is thrown into the pit, producing the characteristic spatial pattern of finds in the fill (*figure 3*, diagram B). The convex shape of the fill is gradually created as the material is repeatedly poured into the pit. Objects find their way into the pit episodically, i.e. when someone intentionally deposits them there. The heavier and larger artefacts typically move down along the sides of the depository cone, causing them to collect in a ring pattern around the middle of the pit. Unlike the natural process of filling, intentional deposition does not end once the pit is full; dumping continues as a result of inertia. An accumulation of deposited material continues to grow where the filled pit is located – this is the so called trash-magnet effect: refuse attracts more refuse (WILK – SCHIFFER 1979, 533). This mass rises naturally above the surrounding terrain and, over time, natural processes cause the material to settle to the ground. These circumstances lead to the frequently documented situation in archaeology in which a large amount (often the majority) of archaeological finds are located on the surface.

The next step was to determine a suitable method that had to be developed for the designated task. The originally planned detailed measurement of all finds using Total Station was tried in 2003 and rejected as ineffective. Ironically, one reason was the method's relative imprecision contrary to expectations (KVĚTINA 2005). This was caused in particular by the inability to maintain the original position of the finds during excavation of loose fill in a feature; as a result the measured coordinates were more or less approximate values. The organization of work was likewise difficult: due to the presence of a single Total Station on the excavated site only one structure could be investigated

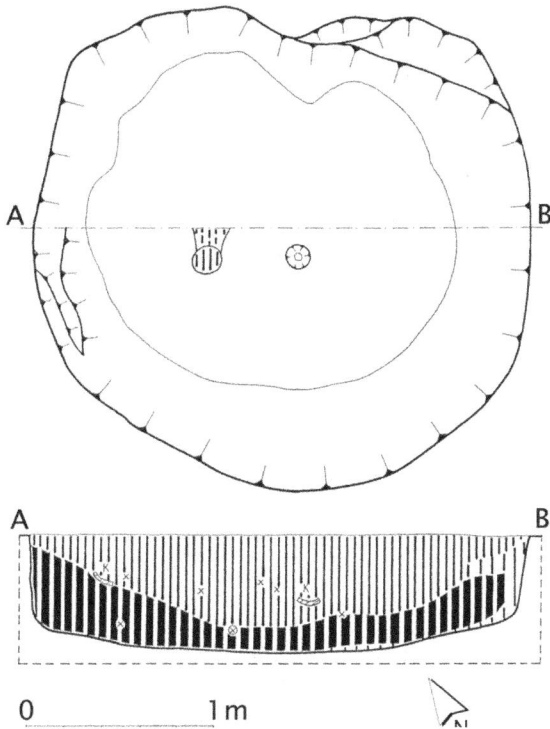

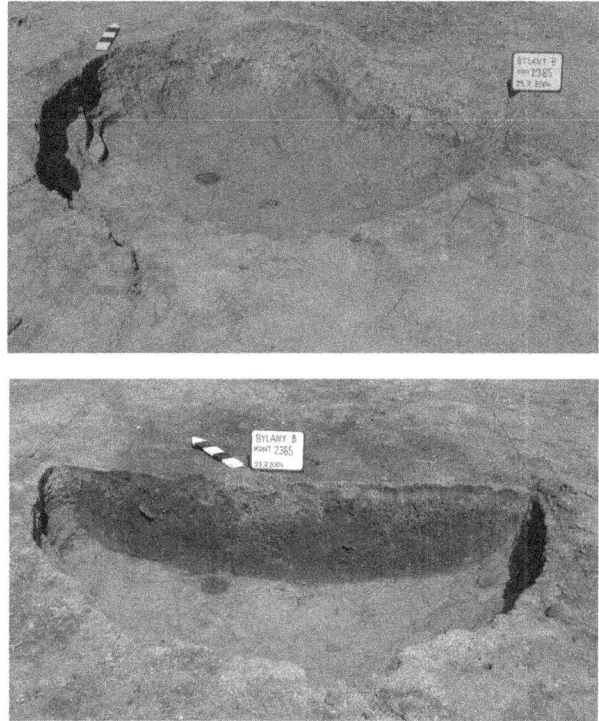

Figure 4. Ground plan and section of feature no. 2385.

at a given time. A different method for recording the position of archaeological finds was therefore tested during rescue excavations in 2004. This method can be referred to as segmented recording, as its principle is based on the simple division of selected archaeological structures into numerous small spatial segments (cubes). The arrangement of the cubes is regular and therefore artificial (it does not respect the natural horizontal or vertical division of

Pottery fragment's properties	Unit of measure
Weight	g
Size	mm
Wall thickness	mm
Shape	four categories
Curvature	mm

Table 1. Studied pottery qualities influencing the formative process of the archaeological material.

features). The dimensions of the cubes used for these purposes depend on the specific conditions, in this particular case 30 x 30 x 10 (depth) cm. During the excavations, the finds were recorded in these spatial cubes; this information was then connected with the finds for the entire processing period.

As an example, we here describe the results of the application of the segmented recording method in feature no. 2385 from the area labeled as "B" during the rescue excavations at the Bylany site in the summer of 2004. The feature had a dimension of 250 x 240 cm x 60 cm, and its original function could not be specified in greater detail. Two post-holes were registered at the bottom of the

feature (*figure 4*). The fill of the feature proved to be homogenous. Pottery fragments from feature no. 2385 were dated to the Late Neolithic (the final phase of the Stroked Pottery culture). Feature no. 2385 contained 368 potsherds (1965 g), 21 stones (2608 g), 1605 g of daub, several animal bones and charcoal concentrations. There were a total of 426 documented sector cubes (71 in the ground plan x 6 vertical layers).

In addition to standard qualities, the pottery also exhibited other parameters hypothetically related to the formation processes of the archaeological material (*table 1*).

The basic tool for spatial analysis of the obtained archaeological data was in this case GIS technology. Its use is standard in today's archaeology, but mainly in analyses at the landscape scale. Intrasite GIS is applied less frequently, and micro-scale spatial analyses involving relationship of the individual artefacts are used very rarely, with the exception of hunter-gatherer archaeology. One of the reasons may be the complicated field of formation processes which complicates spatial analyses. The presented analysis of a Neolithic pit (feature no. 2385) represents one of the possible approaches towards application of GIS methods at the micro-scale.

This spatial analysis of the distribution of archaeological finds was performed in ArcGIS 9.3, including the Spatial Analyst and 3D Analyst extensions. The segmented network of cubes in which the positions of archaeological finds were recorded was created as a polygonal layer, including data on depth (*figure 5*). Each segment was assigned a unique number used to connect the database of

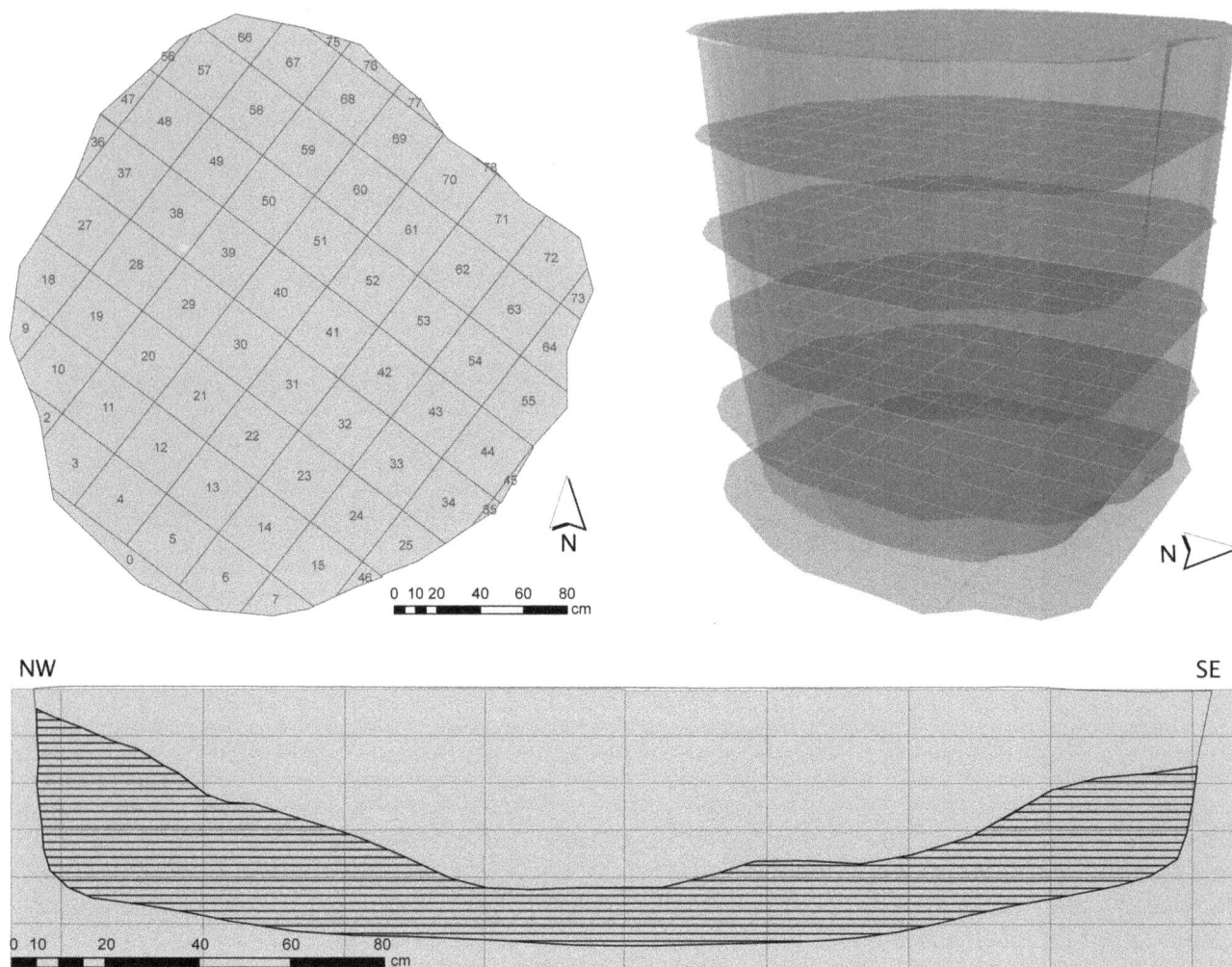

Figure 5. Example of segmental records of feature no. 2385.

archaeological records to the spatial map. The database contained basic quantitative information on all of the finds from feature no. 2385 and more detailed tables on the qualities characterizing the impact of formative processes.

Depth in cm		Pottery	Stones (weight in g)	Daub (weight in g)	Bones	Charcoal
0-10	surface	68	0	108,5	NO	YES
11-20		85	320	194	YES	YES
21-30		78	614	525	NO	YES
31-40		107	389	475	YES	YES
41-50	⊥	23	758	236	YES	YES
51-60	bottom	7	527	66	YES	YES

Table 2. The number of individual categories of archaeo-logical finds with respect to their vertical position.

Spatial distribution was evaluated mainly by empirical observations of the distribution of finds. Above all, we observed a conspicuous accumulation or, to the contrary, dispersion of individual elements. It was found that the greatest concentration of finds from the perspective of their vertical position was located at a depth of 21–40 cm beneath the surface. Concentrations of finds were also relatively steep in the highest layers to a depth of 20 cm

(for pottery quantitatively identical with lower layers). The fewest finds were located in the layers at the bottom. The profile showed that there was also a clear concentration of finds in the northeast part of the feature (*table 2, figure 6*).

The horizontal arrangement of finds in individually studied layers shows an interesting trend: finds did not accumulate in the centre of the studied feature to a depth of 30 cm, but rather in a ring around the centre; from a depth of 31 cm toward the bottom, objects are grouped in the northeast part of the feature (*figure 7*). The horizontal spatial distri-bution of the potsherds in individual artificial layers shows that light potsherds are typically found in the centre of the feature, while heavier potsherds are instead scattered in a ring away from the centre. Unlike their numbers, the verti-cal spatial distribution of the potsherd mass does not show grouping in the northeast part of the feature (*figure 7*). The statistical distribution of potsherd mass by individual lay-ers does not reveal any meaningful pattern (*table 3*).

Another quality analyzed was the S/W index, which is a parameter calculated from the size (S) category of the potsherd and the thickness of the potsherd wall (W). For

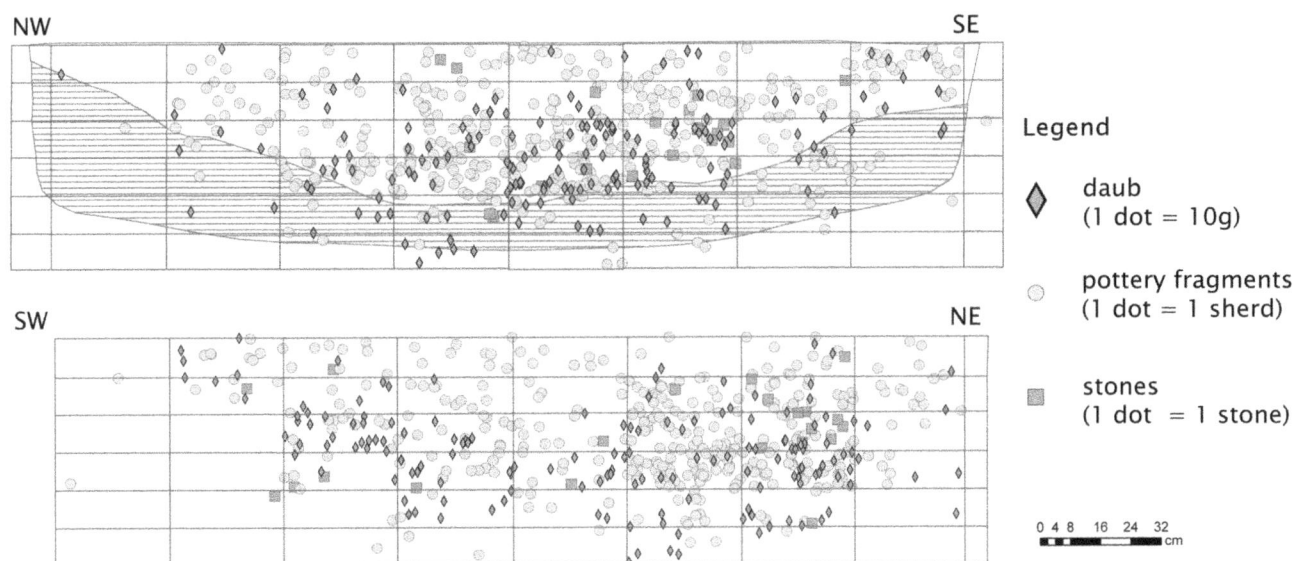

Figure 6. Position of finds in sections. Finds from the whole feature are virtually accumulated in 2D space.

	0-10 cm	11-20 cm	21-30 cm	31-40 cm	41-50 cm	51-60 cm
Min	2	1	3	2	2	4
Quartile 1	8	12.5	10.75	10	8.75	5.5
Quartile 2	11	16.67	16	13.43	15.5	47
Quartile 3	26	31	23.75	17.89	65.5	47
Max	77.5	83	64	48	107	47
Mean	18.12	24.06	19.30	15.73	30.63	21.6

Table 3. Quartiles and mean potsherd weight (in grams).

	0-10 cm	11-20 cm	21-30 cm	31-40 cm	41-50 cm	51-60 cm
Min	3.33	3.54	4.5	3.85	4.05	3.75
Quartile 1	4.8	6.47	5.96	6.19	6.95	5.11
Quartile 2	5.92	7.5	6.95	7.73	7.93	6
Quartile 3	7.55	9.13	8.42	8.65	9.5	11.15
Max	12	10	13.33	13.33	10	12.86
Mean	6	7.09	7.09	7.26	7.30	6.46

Table 4. Quartiles and S/W index parameter means.

Depth in cm	Potsherd curvature in mm			
	3-5	6-8	9-11	>11
0-10	2	2	0	0
11-20	8	1	0	1
21-30	8	2	1	1
31-40	12	3	1	0
41-50	3	0	1	0
51-60	0	0	0	0

Table 5. Frequency of the values of potsherd curvature categories by vertical layers.

example, if the potsherd falls into the 80 mm size category and the thickness of the potsherd's wall is 5 mm, the S/W index value is 16. If a potsherd of the same size has a wall thickness of 10 mm, the S/W index value is 8. This example indicates that the larger the S/W index value, the greater the potsherd's susceptibility toward greater fragmentation. The statistical evaluation of central tendencies and quartiles demonstrates that potsherds from a depth of 11-50 cm have a higher S/W index value. On the other hand, pottery from the top and bottom of the feature has lower values (*table 4*). Nevertheless, the differences between these two groups are not particularly striking.

The horizontal spatial distribution of S/W index values does not reveal any interpretable pattern. The vertical distribution of the S/W index values shows a distinct concentration of higher values in the northeast part of the feature (*figure 8*).

One of the pottery qualities analyzed was potsherd curvature. It is assumed that pottery fragments with more distinct curvature could not withstand the formative processes on the surface for long. This particularly concerns forces such as trampling, burrowing (animals) and blows from other objects which reduce the original large fragments of pottery vessels into small potsherds with minimal curvature. Therefore, if considerably curved pottery fragments are located inside an archaeological feature, it is likely that they were deposited there intentionally (thrown in by a person).

Pottery fragments were divided into categories on the basis of their curvature value (*table 5*). The curvature category could only be evaluated with only 48 out of the total number of 368 potsherds (13%). A spatial analysis of this small amount indicates that potsherds from the category with the highest curvature were not found in either the upper or in the very lower layers of the feature (*table 5*). The potsherds with the greatest curvature occurred at the edges of the artefact fill in the plan view of the feature.

In the same way, the horizontal spatial distribution of daub mass in individual artificial layers shows that the heaviest fragments were not located in the centre of the feature. With the exception of the layer at the depth of 30–40 cm, this also holds true for the middle weight categories (*figure 7*). The same can be said about the weight distribution of stones, despite the fact that this category cannot essentially be evaluated due to the low number of finds in the feature (*figure 7*).

Quantity of pottery

Legend:
- 1
- 2 - 4
- 5 - 8
- 9 - 12
- 13 - 18

Weight of pottery (>10g)

Fragments below
10g not displayed
- 11g - 18g
- 18g - 34g
- 34g - 51g
- 51g - 107g

Weight of daub

Legend:
- 0 - 18g
- 19 - 66g
- 67 - 140g

Weight of stones

Legend:
- 12 - 16g
- 17 - 26g
- 27 - 95g
- 96 - 318g
- 319 - 476g

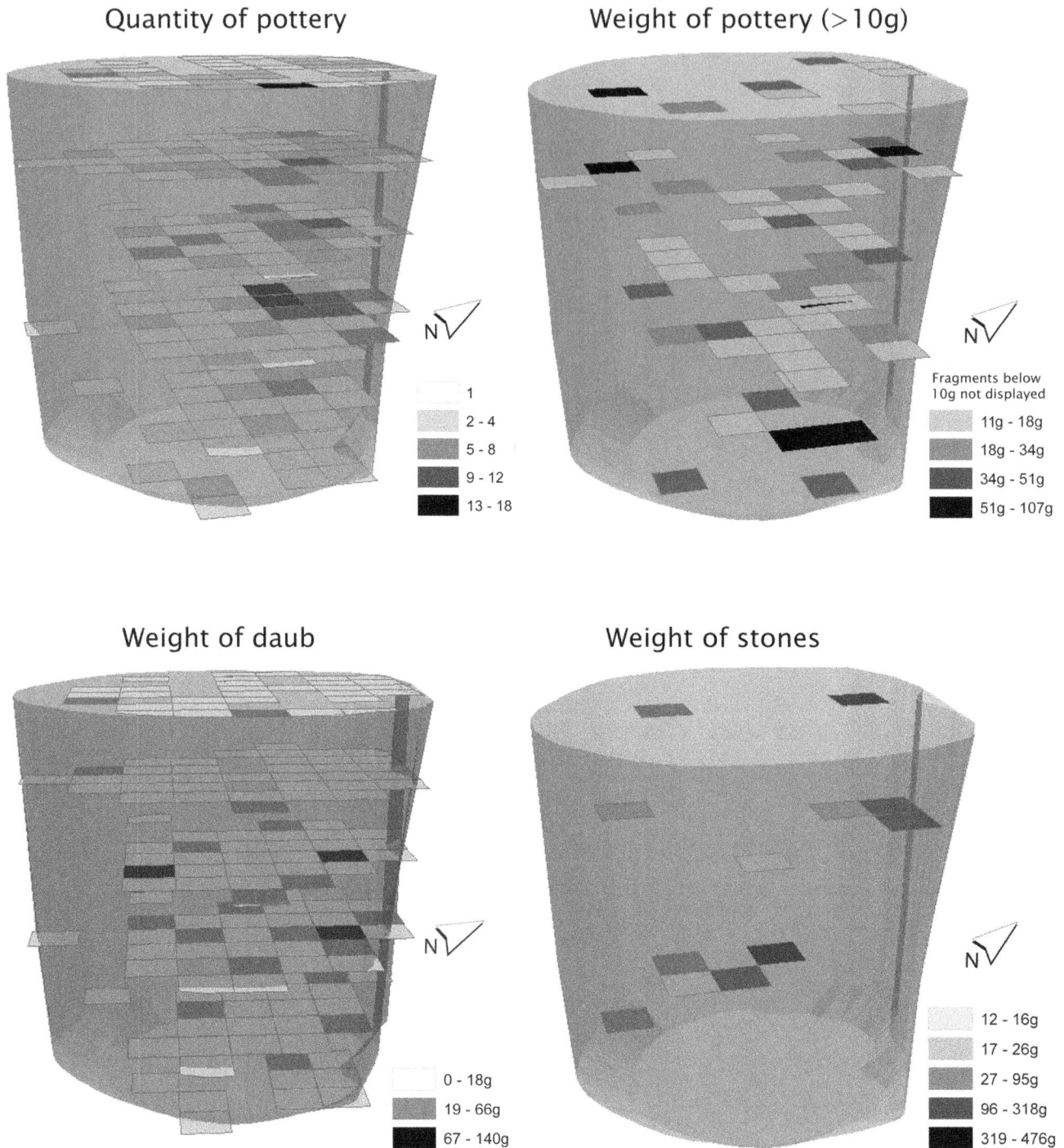

Figure 7. Position, quantity and weight of individual studied categories of finds in a 3D model of the feature. The depth of the feature is doubled for the sake of clarity.

Refitting potsherds

The identification and mapping of the spatial distribution of potsherd refits represents a specific methodical step. Archaeology traditionally defines refits as pottery fragments that can be joined together (glued), proving that they belong to the same pottery vessel. However, the term „refit" has a broader semantic validity. C. BOLLONG most recently systematized refits into six categories (1994, 18). His typology and its application indicate that one refit category also includes fragments that cannot be physically joined

but, according to numerous criteria (technological, formal – various authors use different perspectives), come from a single vessel. This is the category to which the vast majority of the refits from feature no. 2385 belong.

A total of 54 pottery fragments (i.e. 15% of the total number of potsherds) identified in pit no. 2385 could be assigned to more than one vessel. Specifically, these fragments could be assigned to 27 different vessels. *Table 6* presents the frequency of fragments belonging to a single vessel unit. The spatial distribution of these fragments was

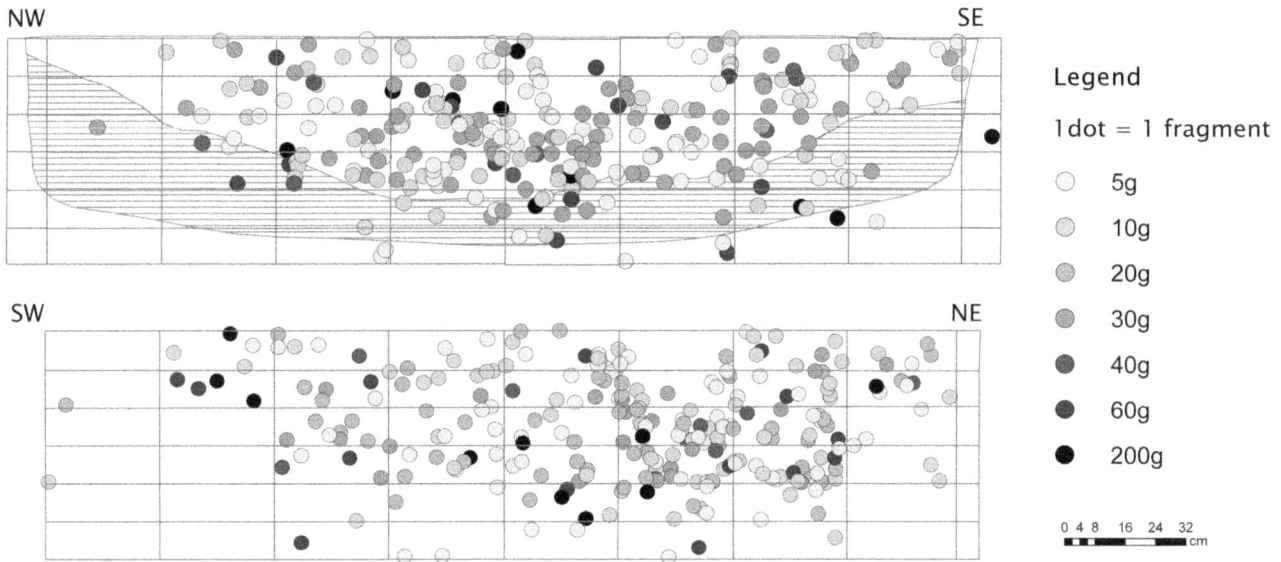

Figure 8. The number and weight of ceramic fragments divided into categories for the two profiles of the feature. The accumulation of potsherds in the NE part of the feature can be seen. Finds from the whole feature are virtually accumulated in 2D space.

the subject of another analysis. A surprisingly high number of the refits (46%) were identified in one spatial cube. We conclude that this involved recent fractures that occurred in the course of the post-deposition processes or even during archaeological excavations themselves. It is also surprising that with the exception of two vessel units (unit nos. 315844 and 315908) the remaining refits are composed of fragment connections between cubes in the same height layer or in two adjacent layers (figure 9). The

average horizontal distance of refit fragments is typically up to 60 cm, the vertical distance up to 15 cm. In other words, the majority of refits are found close to one another. This indicates that larger fragments or even whole vessels were not deposited in the feature; instead, it was smaller fragments of vessel units that had been broken earlier that were placed there.

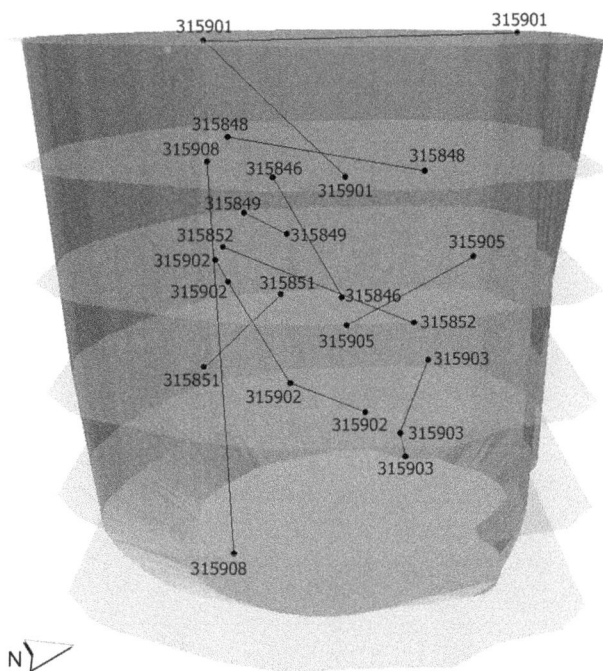

Figure 9. The connecting lines between refits indicate their frequent horizontal and vertical proximity. Vessel unit no. 315844 is not shown. The depth of the feature is doubled for the sake of clarity.

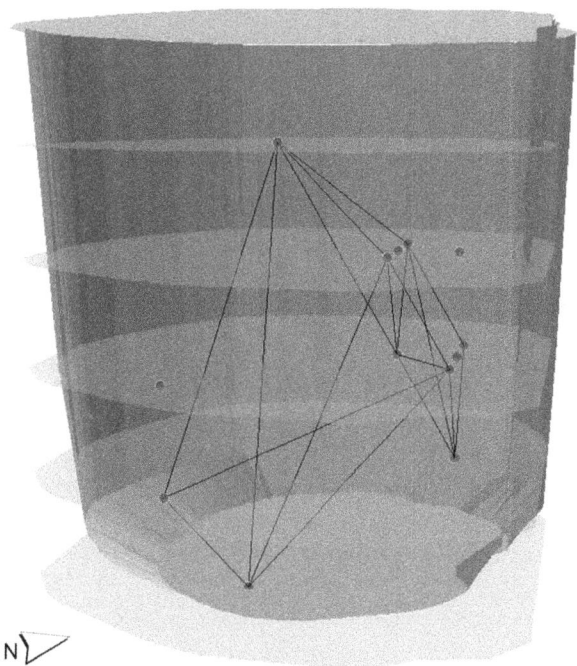

Figure 10. The position of segments containing refits from vessel unit no. 315844 joined using the triangulated irregular network (TIN). The depth of the feature is doubled for the sake of clarity.

Refits among fragments	2	3	4	5	7	33
Frequency	13	5	4	3	1	1

Table 6. Frequency of fragments (refits) belonging to a single vessel unit.

As stated above, there were two exceptions: Unit no. 315908 is composed of two fragments separated by 4 layers (*figure 9*). Unit no. 315844, an entirely unique case, is composed of 33 fragments scattered throughout the entire pit fill. It is their distribution that suggests something about the way the fill in feature no. 2385 originated (*figure 10*). Its position was projected using the structure of a triangulated irregular network (TIN) in the 3D Analyst extension of ArcGIS, which is a very suitable additional tool for spatial analyses and visualization.

Conclusions and interpretation

On the basis of the results we will attempt to formulate an interpretation addressing the primary question of whether the studied archaeological feature was filled intentionally or whether this was the result of subsequent natural processes. The interpretive hypothesis is based on the assumption of two fundamental processes in the creation of a pit fill (unintentional natural and intentional cultural) and were sketched above (*figure 3*). More accurately, the explanation will address the process by which the archaeological finds found their way into pit no. 2385 following the end of its primary function (one that could not be identified in greater detail).

The results of the performed analyses can be divided into two groups. The first group of results is from the spatial analysis of archaeological finds and their parameters tied to formative processes (A). The second group concerns the distribution of refits in the pit fill and the modeling of their origin (B).

A) The greatest concentration of finds in terms of their vertical position was located at a depth of 21–40 cm beneath the surface. The concentration of finds is also relatively high in the highest layer down to a depth of 20 cm. The fewest finds were located in the bottom layer. Objects in the fill have a tendency to group in a ring form around the centre (*figure 7*). Particularly in the lower layers there was also a parallel tendency toward grouping in the NE part of the pit. The pottery qualities referencing formative processes (weight, curvature and SW index) also confirm these trends.

It therefore seems that the interpretation of the spatial localization of the archaeological finds corresponds more to a model of intentional deposition (ring-like grouping and the placement of heavier and larger pieces at the edges of the structure and the relatively high number of finds in the upper layers). On the other hand, the determined accumulation of finds in the NE part of the pit indicates the influence of unintentional runoff: the terrain surrounding feature no. 2385 is sloped to the northeast.

B) The vast majority of refits was localized in a single spatial segment-cube (30 x 30 x 10 cm depth), in segments near to one another or between adjacent vertical layers. The mutual horizontal distance between refits is typically up to 60 cm, the vertical distance up to 15 cm. Vessel unit no. 315908 was exceptional in that potsherds were 40 cm apart. Vessel unit no. 315844, whose individual fragments were scattered throughout the entire pit, was an entirely unique case.

Vessel unit no. 315844 serves as a good model for interpreting the formative processes. If we assume that a greater number of fragments from a single vessel unit reached the pit as the result of a specific event that occurred within a short time interval, the distribution of these fragments should provide information on the form of the pit's fill at that particular time. Figure 10 shows the position of segments containing pottery fragments from vessel unit no. 315844. The shape that the connected fragments form using the triangulated irregular network (TIN) structure is decidedly convex. This indicates that in the period in which the fragments found their way into the pit, the fill had the appearance of a depository cone, along whose walls the pottery fragments were spread.

The depository history of pit no. 2385 apparently reflects a series of events that are mostly the result of intentional human activity. The artefacts probably reached the pit as a type of secondary refuse that was substantially fine and fragmented. In the case of pottery this means that broken, but whole, vessels were reused as much as possible before being discarded, so only relatively small parts were dumped in the pit in the end. The pit fill, which was created as an intentional part of the refuse strategy at the settlement, was then subjected to natural post-deposition processes. For example, these forces caused finds to collect in the steeper parts lower down the pit.

One of the goals of the project was to test the possibilities of GIS technology in dealing with the formation processes of the archaeological record. Standard user-defined parameters of feature projection in geographical space were applied at the micro-scale. The "space" in this case consisted of an underground archaeological feature. The final results of the analyses validated the expected potential of GIS for micro-scale study of spatial properties. 3D projection methods proved valuable in achieving the goals defined, in contrast to the classical use of GIS methods in archaeology.

References Cited

BOLLONG, C. A. 1994: Analysis of the stratigraphy and formation processes using patterns of pottery sherd dispersion, *Journal of Field Archaeology* 21, 15 – 28.

DEAL, M. 1985: Household Pottery Disposal in the Maya Highlands: An Ethnoarchaeological Interpretation, *Journal of Anthropology and Archaeology* 4, 243 – 291.

DEBOER, W. R. – LATHRAP, D. W. 1979: The making and breaking of Shipibo-Conibo ceramics. In: Krammer, C. (ed.): *Ethnoarchaeology implications of ethnography for archaeology,* New York, 102 – 138.

GRAHAM, M. 1994: *Mobile Farmers. An Ethnoarchaeological Approach to Settlement Organization among the Rarámuri of Northwestern Mexico,* Ann Arbor.

HAYDEN, B. – CANNON, A. 1983: Where the Garbage Goes: Refuse Disposal in the Maya Highlands, *Journal of anthropological archaeology* 2, 117 – 163.

CHAPMAN, J. – GAYDARSKA, B. 2007: *Parts and Wholes: Fragmentation in Prehistoric Context,* Oxford.

KVĚTINA, P. 2005: Možnosti mikroprostorové analýzy artefaktů v archeologických objektech. In: Pavlů, I. (ed.): *Bylany Varia 3,* Prague, 9 – 16.

KVĚTINA, P.(in print): The spatial analysis of non-ceramic refuse from the Neolithic site at Bylany, Czech Republic, *European Journal of Archaeology.*

KVĚTINA, P. – PAVLŮ, I. 2007: *Neolitické sídliště v Bylanech – základní databáze, (*Neolithic settlement at Bylany – essential database),* Prague.

LAST, J. 1998: The Residue of Yesterday's Existence: Settlement Space and Discard at Miskovice and Bylany. In: Pavlů, I. (ed.): *Bylany Varia 1,* Prague, 17 – 45.

MIDGLEY, M. – PAVLŮ, I. – RULF, J. – ZÁPOTOCKÁ, M. 1993: Fortified settlements or ceremonial sites: new evidence from Bylany, Czechoslovakia, *Antiquity* 67/254, 91 – 96.

PAVLŮ, I. 2000: *Life on a Neolithic site.* Prague.

PAVLŮ, I. – RULF, J. – ZÁPOTOCKÁ, M. 1986: Theses on the Neolithic Site of Bylany, *Památky archeologické* 77, 288 – 412.

PAVLŮ, I. – RULF, J. – ZÁPOTOCKÁ, M. 1995: Bylany Rondel. Model of the Neolithic Site, Praehistorica Archaeologica Bohemica 1995, *Památky archeologické – Supplementum* 3, 7 – 123.

PAVLŮ, I. – ZÁPOTOCKÁ, M. 1978: *Analysis of the Czech Neolithic Pottery. Projection, Handles and Spouts,* Prague.

PAVLŮ, I. – ZÁPOTOCKÁ, M. 1983: *Bylany. Katalog A-1,* Prague.

PAVLŮ, I. – ZÁPOTOCKÁ, M. – SOUDSKÝ, O. 1985: *Bylany. Katalog A-2,* Prague.

PAVLŮ, I. – ZÁPOTOCKÁ, M. – SOUDSKÝ, O. 1987: *Bylany. Katalog B, F,* Prague.

PEŠKE, L. – RULF, J. – SLAVÍKOVÁ, J. 1998: Bylany – ekodata. Specifikace nálezů kostí a rostlinných makrozbytků. In: Pavlů, I. (ed.): *Bylany Varia 1,* Prague, 83 – 117.

RULF, J. (ed.) 1989: *Bylany Seminar 1987. Collected papers.* Prague.

SOUDSKÝ, B. 1962: The Neolithic site of Bylany, *Antiquity* 36/173, 190 – 200.

SOUDSKÝ, B. 1967. *Principles of automatic data treatment applied on Neolithic pottery,* Prague, (manuscript of the Institute of Archaeology CAS, Prague).

SOUDSKÝ, B. – PAVLŮ, I. 1972: The Linear Pottery Culture settlements patterns of Central Europe. In: Ucko, P. J. – Tringham, R. – Dimbleby, G. W. (eds.): *Man, settlement and urbanism,* London, 317 – 328.

WILK, R. – SCHIFFER, M. 1979: The archaeology of Vacant Lots in Tucson, Arizona, *American Antiquity* 44/3, 520 – 536.

Petr Květina
Institute of Archaeology CAS, Prague, v.v.i.
Letenská 4,
118 01 – Prague 1
Czech Republic
kvetina@arup.cas.cz

Markéta Končelová
Institute of Archaeology CAS, Prague, v.v.i.
Letenská 4,
118 01 – Prague 1
Czech Republic
koncelova@arup.cas.cz

P. Verhagen, A. G. Posluschny, A. Danielisová (eds.)
Proceedings EAA 2009: Go Your Own Least Cost Path, Riva del Garda

Pyrotechnology or Fires.
Spatial Analysis of Overfired Pottery from the Late Bronze Age Settlement in Turnov – Maškovy Zahrady (NE Bohemia)

Richard Thér, Jan Prostředník

Abstract

A high proportion of overfired pottery is a characteristic phenomenon of pottery assemblages from Late Bronze Age settlements in Eastern Bohemia. The amount of overfired pottery is incomparable with any other prehistoric period. Accidental fires do not seem to be an adequate explanation of the phenomenon. Spatial analysis has been used to test the hypothesis that overfired pottery is a consequence of systemic behavior: the secondary use of sherds in pottery firing technology. This hypothesis has been supported by experimental research. The settlement in Turnov-Maškovy zahrady (NE Bohemia) revealed a spatial pattern that could be used for modeling the spatial consequences of this hypothesis. The analysis has revealed a spatial correlation between clusters of postholes and the distribution of the overfired pottery at the site. The significant presence of overfired pottery in the assemblage is therefore probably due to settlement fires rather than to firing technology. The intentional destruction of houses by fire seems to be a plausible explanation of the phenomenon.

Introduction

A high proportion of overfired pottery[1] seems to be a characteristic phenomenon of ceramic assemblages from Late Bronze Age settlements in Eastern Bohemia. This phenomenon has not been a subject of systematic study up to now. Based on the authors' observation of ceramic assemblages from the region, the amount of Late Bronze Age overfired pottery seems to be incomparable with any other prehistoric period in the region. The phenomenon is usually interpreted as a consequence of settlement fires (e.g. SKLENÁŘOVÁ 2005 for the settlement in Turnov - Maškovy zahrady), but accidental fires (hypothesis A) do not seem to be an adequate explanation of the phenomenon. The regularity and extension of the phenomenon leads to the consideration that there must have been a systematic behavior behind the occurrence of overfired pottery in the Late Bronze Age.

---

[1] The occurrence of the overfired pottery depends on the heating rate, clay properties and firing temperature. From a mineralogical point of view the overfired pottery is characterized in this case by the presence of an amorphous glassy phase and by the presence of fast spherical voids. During fast heating forced by high temperatures (ranging from 900 –1000 °C), the crystal structure of clay minerals breaks down, causing the fluid phase to escape and create spherical voids. At higher temperatures (1000–1100°C) the clay minerals start to melt and the proportion of the amorphous glassy phase increases.

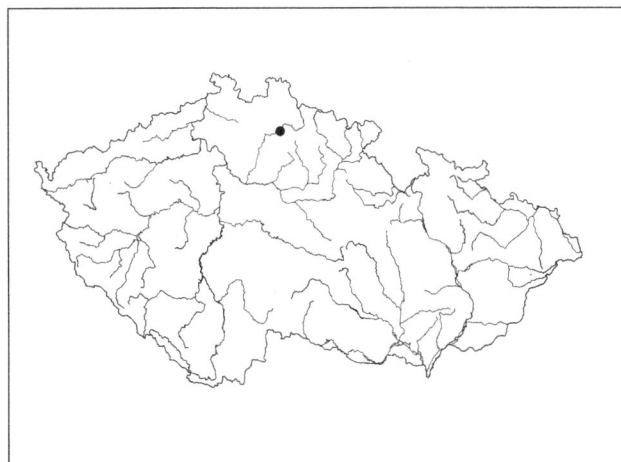

Figure. 1. Location of Turnov-Maškovy zahrady

The alternative explanation (hypothesis B) assumes that the overfired pottery is a consequence of the pyrotechnology used. This pyrotechnology should meet two presumptions: A) It was a common component of settlement economy and B) it has the potential to cause the overfiring effects on pottery. The only pyrotechnology that meets these presumptions in the context of Late Bronze Age settlements is pottery technology. Overfiring on a regular basis can be caused by reusing ceramic sherds in a pottery firing. Sherds used as separators between pottery load and fuel or as isolators of firing are exposed to the highest temperatures and extreme heating rates in a firing. The applied firing procedures have been thermally variable and could locally considerably exceed 1000°C. The repeated use of sherds will have increased the probability of overfiring and in consequence it will have increased the proportion of overfired pottery in the assemblage. Experiments have proved that the secondary use of sherds in pottery firing technology causes a significant increase of the overfired pottery proportion in a pottery refuse. After five experimental pottery firings 25% of the reused sherds showed apparent signs of overfiring (THÉR 2009). Both hypotheses were tested by a spatial analysis of pottery attributes in the context of the Late Bronze Age settlement of Turnov - Maškovy zahrady.

Archaeological situation

The site selected for the spatial analysis - Turnov - Maškovy zahrady - is situated in the northeastern part of Bohemia (*figure 1*). The eastern part of the excavated area revealed an interesting spatial pattern. Relatively large features with a concentration of ceramic and daub fragments (254, 117, 15, and 1/C6/A) are distributed in a regular pattern with

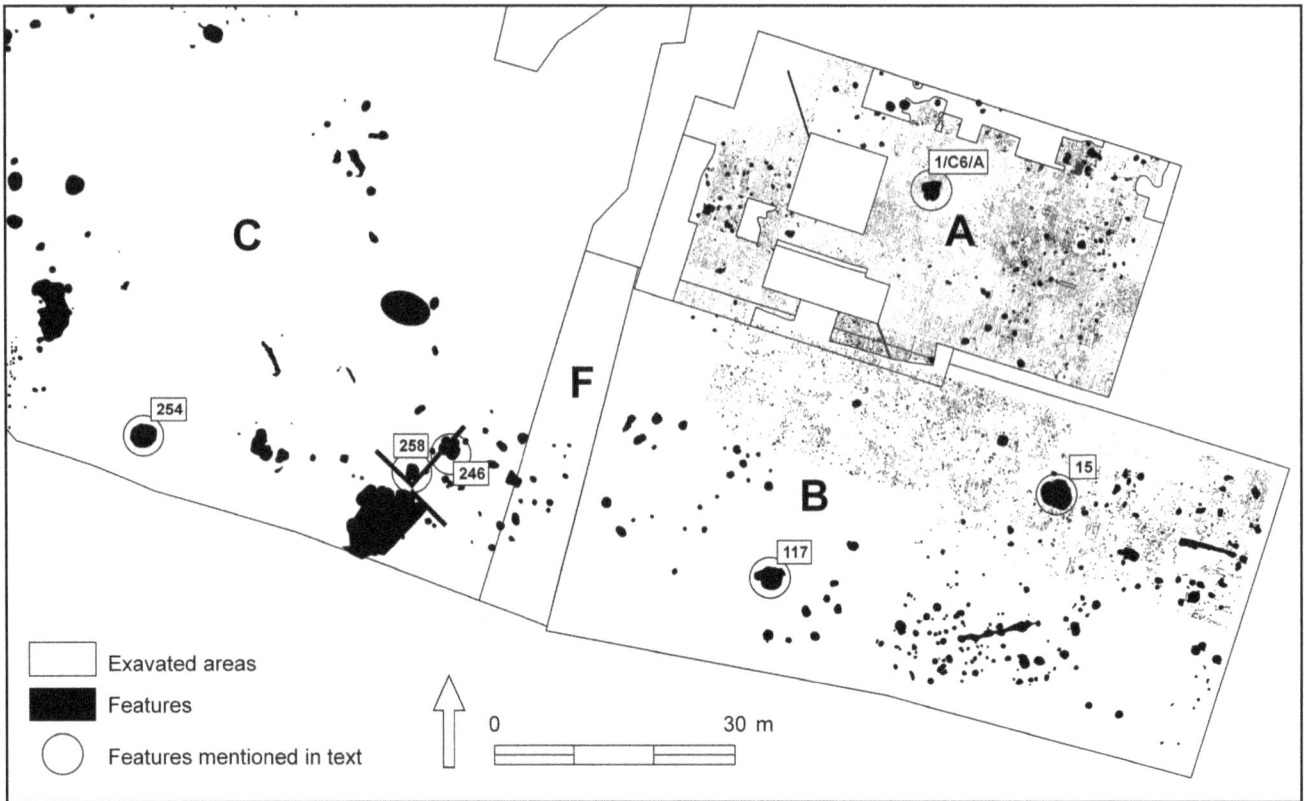

Figure. 2. Eastern part of the excavated area (Turnov - Maškovy zahrady).

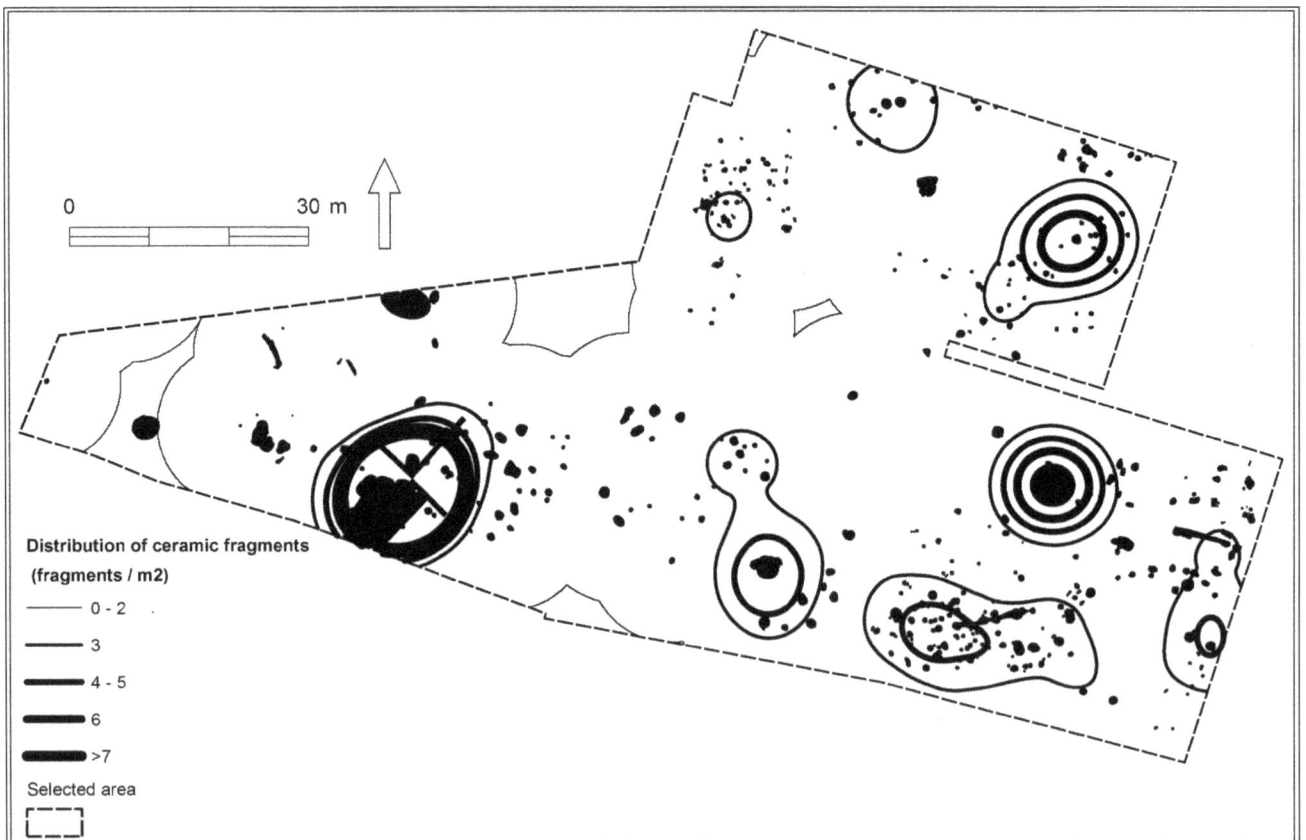

Figure. 3. Distribution of ceramic fragments in the selected area.

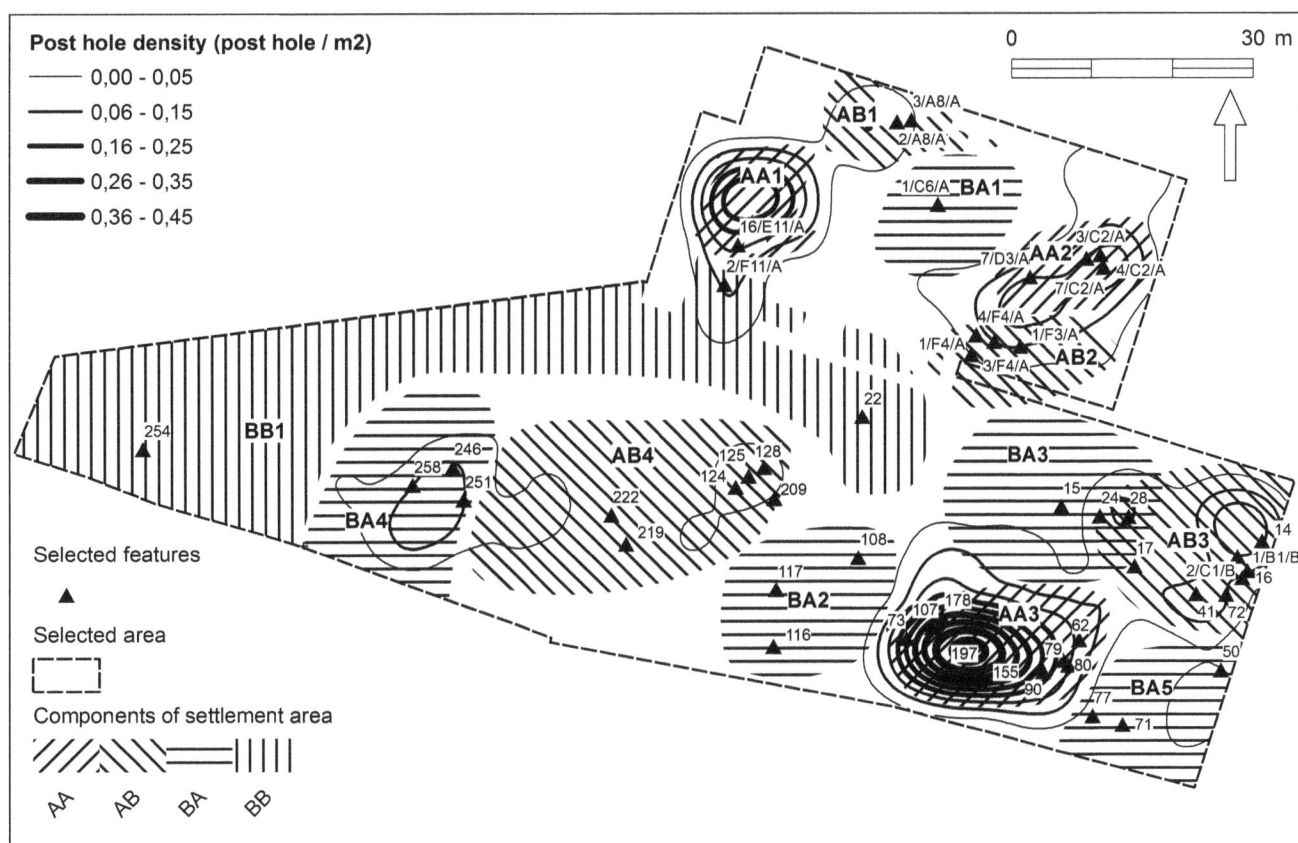

Figure. 4. Hypothetical functional components of settlement area in the selected area.

similar distances between the features (approx. 30 m). The features are surrounded by clusters of postholes (*figure 2*). The pottery assemblage in the areas of analysis was dated to the Bronze Age D – Hallstatt B periods, and 40% of the pottery assemblage weight is overfired. The occupation of the eastern part of the excavation area provides a good basis for an analysis of space utilization because there is a strong continuity of the spatial pattern during the existence of the settlement. Further west the Late Bronze Age occupation is mixed with Late Hallstatt, Roman and Early Slavonic occupation (BLÁHOVÁ-SKLENÁŘOVÁ – PROSTŘEDNÍK 2007A; 2007B; DROBERJAR – PROSTŘEDNÍK 2004; 1999; 2001; 2002; SKLENÁŘOVÁ 2005). These parts of the excavated area were excluded from the analysis.

The settlement in the selected area is located on a gentle west-facing slope, which is bounded to the west by the edge of an alluvial terrace. Nowadays, this very smooth transition is evident from an increased slope. Features in the southern part of this area either contained the Late Bronze Age pottery or they did not reveal chronologically significant artifacts. There are no remains of buildings in this area. The cluster of small postholes on the southern edge of the area is different from the remains of the Late Bronze Age buildings in the other parts of the excavation and presumably represents a functionally different structure, e.g. a fence. In spite of the presence of the features, there is a very low density of pottery debris in the area (*figure 3*). The absence of buildings and the low debris concentration could mark a settlement periphery. Occa-

sional activities perceived as dangerous for buildings or inhabitants, such as pottery firing, could have taken place within this zone.

The model of technological behavior and its consequences

The important question is whether we can assume that a restricted space for pottery firing technology existed which could leave archaeologically detectable traces or influence the composition of pottery assemblages. Pottery production may be organized as either a flexible activity or as one that assumes a more spatially restricted structure (ARNOLD III 1991, 100–109). In the case of Late Bronze Age pottery production, we assume household production mode, seasonality, and low production output (THÉR 2009). At this level of production there should be little investment in production tools and almost no occurrence of immobile facilities. As a result, spatially demanding activities (such as vessel drying) and residue producing activities (such as firing) should also be located in a flexible fashion. The only rule for the placing of pottery firings was a sufficient distance from domestic structures to prevent settlement fires as is suggested by ethnographic data (ARNOLD 1978; ARNOLD III 1991, 109-113; DEBOER – LANTHARP 1979, 124; LONGACRE 1981, 60; TSCHOPIK 1950; WAANE 1977). Pottery firings could have been placed in open yards between buildings or in a settlement periphery.

Ft	Com	A	B	C	D	E	F	G	H	I	J
14	AB	0,0	0,3	1,4	0,3	1,8	3,7	1,7	0,0	0,6	1
15	BA	0,2	1,2	0,5	0,9	1,9	0,2	0,4	7,8	1,8	3
16	AB	0,4	0,3	0,8	0,6	0,5	0,1	0,0	0,5	1,3	1
17	AB	0,2	0,5	2,6	1,0	0,5	0,0	0,0	1,8	1,2	1
22	BB	0,1	0,9	0,4	0,9	2,1	0,2	0,0	0,7	1,3	1
24	AB	0,3	0,5	0,0	0,4	0,2	0,4	0,2	0,2	0,6	1
28	AB	0,4	0,5	0,8	0,8	0,3	0,3	0,1	0,3	0,6	1
41	AB	0,0	1,0	0,0	1,1	0,6	0,2	0,2	0,4	0,6	1
50	BA	0,1	0,9	2,2	0,6	1,4	0,4	0,1	0,8	2,4	2
62	AA	2,3	0,5	0,1	1,4	0,3	0,2	0,4	1,2	1,3	1
71	BA	0,0	0,7	1,2	1,1	1,0	0,7	0,4	0,6	0,7	2
72	AB	0,0	0,5	0,5	0,9	0,8	1,0	2,0	0,6	0,4	1
73	AA	0,5	0,8	0,4	0,9	0,8	0,3	0,3	1,4	1,0	2
77	BA	0,1	0,8	1,3	0,8	0,9	0,6	0,4	0,4	1,1	3
79	AA	0,0	0,3	5,7	1,3	0,7	0,4	1,1	0,1	0,7	2
80	AA	0,0	1,0	0,3	0,7	2,6	0,0	0,2	0,7	1,5	2
90	AA	2,5	1,4	0,5	1,0	1,1	0,2	0,6	0,9	1,6	2
107	AA	1,3	1,4	0,4	1,9	0,1	0,2	4,9	0,5	0,7	1
108	BA	0,0	1,0	4,1	1,7	1,0	0,4	0,3	1,0	0,5	3
116	BA	0,3	0,5	0,5	0,8	0,9	0,2	0,8	1,1	1,7	3
117	BA	0,1	0,5	0,9	1,0	0,8	0,2	0,6	5,4	1,2	3
124	AB	0,0	0,3	1,5	1,2	0,8	0,6	0,8	0,5	1,2	2
125	AB	0,2	0,6	1,2	0,6	1,0	0,2	0,3	0,6	1,2	2
128	AB	0,2	0,7	0,0	0,4	1,7	0,4	0,2	0,2	0,9	1
155	AA	2,1	1,3	0,1	0,6	0,9	1,3	0,6	0,4	0,6	1
178	AA	0,5	0,9	0,1	0,7	0,5	0,2	0,3	0,6	1,0	2
197	AA	0,5	0,6	0,8	1,0	0,8	16,3	16,9	0,1	0,6	1
209	AB	0,1	0,7	1,6	0,7	1,2	0,3	0,2	0,7	1,1	1
219	AB	0,9	0,3	0,6	0,7	0,8	0,4	0,5	0,9	0,8	2
222	AB	0,1	0,8	1,0	1,1	1,8	0,2	0,5	1,0	1,0	1
246	BA	0,0	0,8	0,6	1,0	1,3	0,2	0,6	1,3	1,2	3
251	BA	0,0	0,7	0,2	1,2	2,7	0,4	0,7	0,4	0,7	2
254	BB	0,4	0,5	2,2	1,1	0,9	0,0	0,5	5,5	1,0	2
258	BA	0,2	0,8	0,8	0,7	0,9	1,1	0,8	2,0	0,3	1
1/B1/B	AB	0,0	0,5	0,0	0,4	1,8	0,1	0,1	0,6	1,1	2
1/C6/A	BA	0,2	0,9	0,4	1,1	0,2	0,1	0,2	3,3	1,2	3
1/F3/A	AB	0,0	0,7	1,6	1,0	0,6	0,9	0,4	0,3	1,1	1
1/F4/A	AB	0,2	0,3	0,0	1,4	0,7	0,1	1,4	0,5	0,7	2
16/E11/A	AA	0,1	0,9	0,3	1,7	0,7	7,1	0,5	0,2	0,6	1
2/A8/A	AB	1,8	1,4	0,9	2,1	0,2	0,5	0,5	0,9	0,9	1
2/C1/B	AB	0,0	0,2	1,6	0,6	0,4	0,1	0,0	0,3	1,1	2
2/F11/A	BB	0,8	1,4	0,0	0,4	2,4	0,4	1,5	0,2	1,0	1
3/A8/A	AB	0,6	0,6	1,2	1,4	0,5	0,3	0,3	0,9	1,1	3
3/C2/A	AA	2,8	1,0	2,4	1,7	0,0	1,2	0,5	0,2	0,6	1
3/F4/A	AB	0,2	0,2	1,9	1,0	1,1	0,2	0,0	0,5	0,9	1
4/C2/A	AA	2,7	0,4	0,3	1,8	0,0	1,2	4,0	0,1	0,7	1
4/F4/A	AB	0,0	0,5	0,0	0,8	0,0	3,2	0,4	0,0	0,3	1
7/C2/A	AA	2,0	1,1	0,3	1,0	0,2	0,9	1,6	0,7	2,0	3
7/D3/A	AA	2,9	1,7	1,9	1,4	0,8	1,2	0,1	0,4	0,9	1

Table 1. Attributes of the features selected for the analysis.

Hypotheses of spatial organization of pottery technology should be based on plans of synchronic settlement phases and respect the dynamics of settlement history. Unfortunately, Late Bronze Age settlement remains usually do not allow for the differentiating of particular settlement phases. In spite of these difficulties the model can be built on the assumption that the same behavioral patterns and resulting spatial structure of activities were replicated during the settlement history. If a continuity of space utilization was maintained during the settlement's history and the activity areas were not gradually mixed together (as seems to be in the case of the eastern part of the site), each area can be separated and archaeological remains found within this area can be analyzed as being the result of past behavior within the area.

In the context of the analyzed area four types of spatial components were defined (*figure 4*).
- Type AA represents clusters of postholes with a density of more than 0.1 posthole / m². Building plans can be reconstructed at least partially in the area. These areas represent the remains of main settlement buildings, probably residential buildings, and their close vicinity. Type AB consists of postholes and other pits. The number of postholes is indicative for the presence of buildings, but the density of postholes is low. AB areas may represent areas with different types of (nonresidential) buildings, or the same activity areas as type AA with different depositional and/or postdepositional histories.
- Type BA represents areas without remains of buildings but with larger irregular pits (117, 15, 1/C6/A) containing a number of pottery sherds and daub. These areas may represent open places in the vicinity of houses and other buildings intended for complex daily based economic and/or social activities including some kind of pyrotechnology (probably mainly food processing).
- Type BB is characterized by a low density of pottery debris and the absence of buildings. Feature 254 in this area is similar to those in type BA areas (117, 15, 1/C6/A). The area can be considered as the settlement periphery, distant from buildings and refuse areas. This area could have been used for spatially extensive activities and/or activities necessarily located at a sufficient distance from buildings like pottery firings. However, pottery firings could also have been located in BA areas.

Consequences of the model
The pottery firing technology model does not predict an unusual concentration of pottery debris because of its hypothetic spatial flexibility, but it can be assumed to produce a specific composition of pottery debris.
1. The repeated use of sherds in pottery firing technology increases the probability of overfiring and in consequence it increases the proportion of overfired pottery in BB and/or BA areas.
2. The secondary use of sherds in firing technology is selective. Plain and large sherds are preferred. Con-

sequently, there will be a higher proportion of sherds from bowls, lower parts of vessels and large vessels in the BB and/or the BA areas.

Materials and methods

The entire ceramic assemblage from the selected area comprises 11,579 ceramic fragments. For the analysis only features containing more than 20 ceramic fragments were selected to exclude small ceramic assemblages from quantification of the attribute proportions. Unfortunately, the selected features are not evenly spaced across the analyzed area leaving large unsampled areas. Features on the borders of these areas have a strong influence on predicted values. This effect has to be considered during the interpretation.

Each ceramic fragment (n = 7,125) from the selected features was characterized according to the following series of attributes (*table 1*):

Attributes related to the consequences of the tested hypothesis
A) Proportion of overfired pottery.
B) Proportion of large vessel fragments (volume > 20 l; volume was estimated using a regression equation based on dependence of vessel volume on wall thickness measured on entire vessel).
C) Proportion of vessel base fragments.

Formative processes attributes
D) Average fragmentation index (*FI = actual ceramic fragment weight / average ceramic fragment weight for given wall thickness in entire assemblage*; a higher index means less fragmentation (KUNA – PROFANTOVÁ 2005, 123) – this variable is used instead of the traditional FI defined by M. SCHIFFER (1996, 283) due to the degree of assemblage fragmentation).
E) Proportion of heavily abraded pottery (if the shape of a sherd is rounded, most of the original surface is not preserved; overfired fragments were excluded because they are more susceptible to abrasion and all of them show attributes of heavily abraded pottery).
F) Ceramic fragment density (*ceramic fragments / m³ of feature fill*; feature fill volume is estimated using 3D modeling in AutoCAD Civil 3D based on feature plans and sections).
G) Daub density (*daub weight / m³ of feature fill*).

Feature attributes
H) Area of feature surface (based on 2D projection of feature plan).
I) Average feature depth (based on documented feature sections).
J) Stratigraphic complexity (ordinal scale based on the number of distinguished stratigraphical units).
The attributes (except stratigraphic complexity) are expressed as indices representing the ratio between the attribute value of a particular feature, and the attribute value

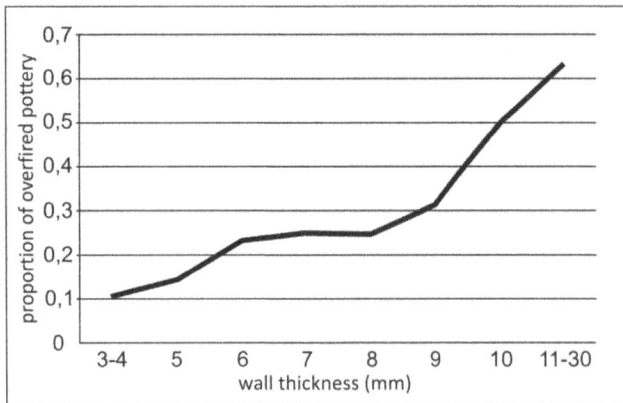

Figure. 5. Dependence of the proportion of overfired pottery on wall thickness.

of the whole assemblage from the selected area. The ratio emphasizes the variability in the spatial distribution of attributes.

The spatial analysis was based on the assumption that the feature deposits are samples which were created by cultural and natural processes. The composition of residues is strongly influenced by nearby activities and is not related directly to the feature's function. Feature attributes were incorporated in the quantitative analysis to test this assumption. If the assumption is valid, than there is no correlation between a feature's morphology and its proportion of particular pottery attribute values.

Categorical principal components analysis (CATPCA) was used to reduce the complexity of the multivariate data

and describes the relations between the analyzed attributes. CATPCA uses optimal scaling to generalize the principal components analysis procedure so that it can accommodate variables of mixed measurement levels (MEULMAN ET AL. 2004). The standard principal components analysis assumes linear relationships between numerical variables. This assumption is not met in the case of the analyzed data. The optimal-scaling approach allows variables to be scaled at different levels.

Spatial analysis was performed using ArcGIS Desktop and its extension Spatial Analyst. The database was joined to the excavation plan. Polygons of the selected features were converted to points placed in polygon centroids. The points served as input data for interpolation and density calculations. The basic interpolation method was inverse distance weighted (IDW) interpolation. IDW estimates unknown values by averaging the values of sample data points in the vicinity of each cell. The closer a point is to the center of the cell being estimated, the more influence it has in the averaging process (MCCOY ET AL. 2002, 136–138). This algorithm broadly corresponds to the presumed effects of formation processes. It allows estimating surface distribution of artifacts as a consequence of local activity. IDW as a deterministic method is more suitable for this type of analysis than geostatistical methods that are based on statistical models that include autocorrelation. Geostatistical methods assume that data is spatially autocorrelated. But it can be predicted that at least some of the data is not spatially autocorrelated because:
- An excavation plan is a mix of different synchronic levels and thus a mix of different processes with their own spatially structured consequences.

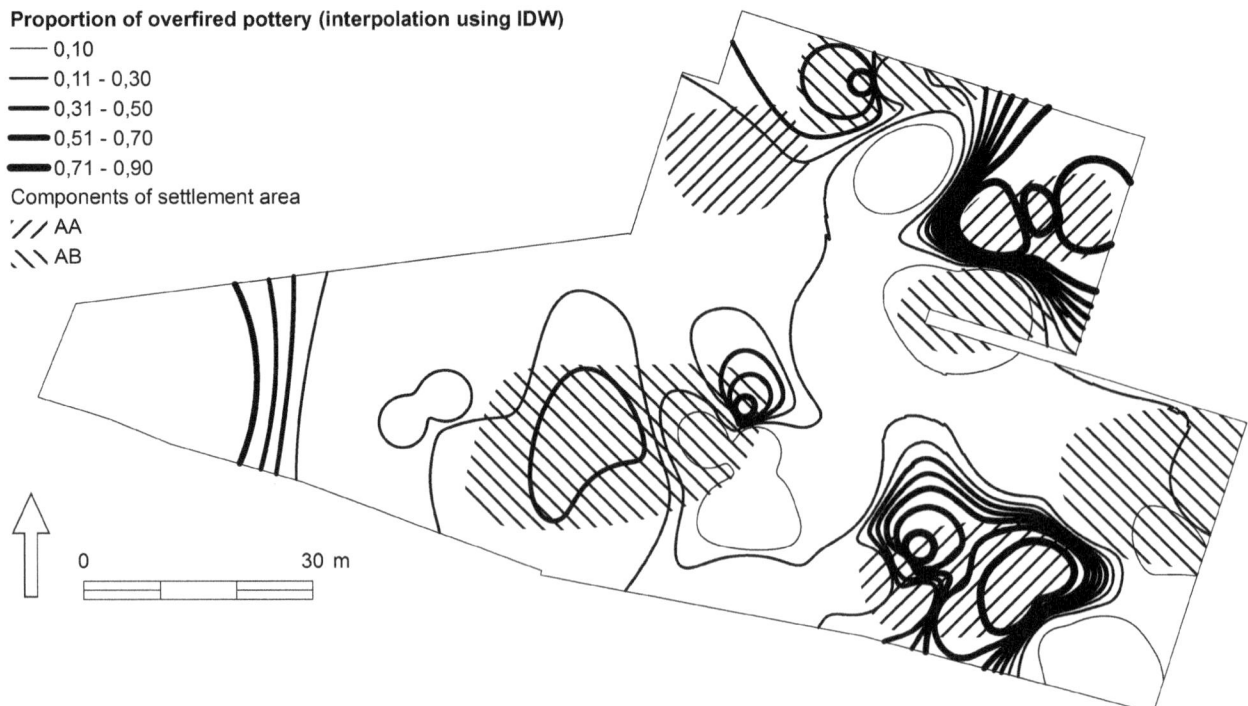

Figure. 6. IDW interpolation of overfired pottery distribution.

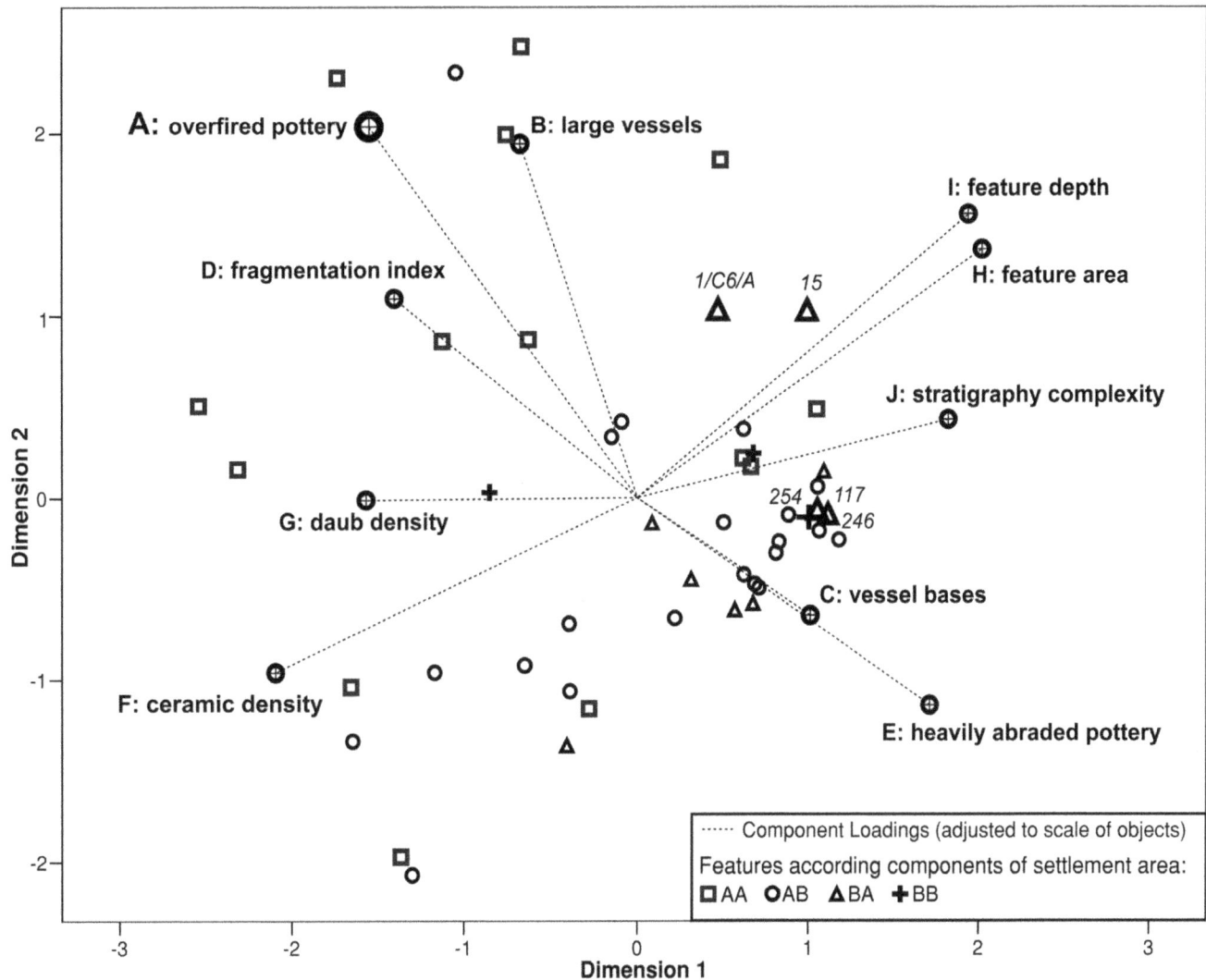

Figure. 7. CATPCA - biplot of object scores and component loadings.

- There could be archeologically undetected barriers (fences, walls, ...) that prevented the spreading of artifacts.
- Human behavior strongly influenced the depositional processes.

Therefore, fitting a predictive model based on spatial autocorrelation is not an appropriate approach. The interpretation of interpolated surfaces is based on assessing surface morphology and is an intuitive task. Plain surfaces imply homogeneity and continuity of space utilization, while a dramatic morphology of the surface can reveal a complicated history of the area with discontinuities. Surfaces can also help to reveal the chronological relation between features or unknown barriers.

Results

Overfired pottery was the attribute of primary interest. Traces of overfiring were observed on 26% of the ceramic fragments which represents 40% of the assemblage weight. The proportion of overfired pottery increases with wall thickness. More than half of the fragments thicker than 10 mm is overfired (*figure 5*). This evident trend could reflect selectivity which conforms to hypothesis B. However, we can find another possible cause of the trend. Overfired sherds are more susceptible to abrasion, so thinner sherds have less chance to survive the effects of formative processes.

According to the spatial analysis, overfired pottery evidently concentrates in AA areas. Less and uneven concentrations can be observed in AB areas. In BA areas the concentration of overfired pottery is far below average. Higher values in area BB1 are caused by the influence of feature 254 (*figure 6*).

The results of the CATPCA analysis show the relations between the selected variables. The first two dimensions explain 52% of data variability. These dimensions create the axes of the biplot of objects and component loadings (*figure 7*). The vector of a variable points into the direction of the highest value of the variable. Longer vectors account for more data variance than the shorter ones. The relations between the variables are represented by their location in

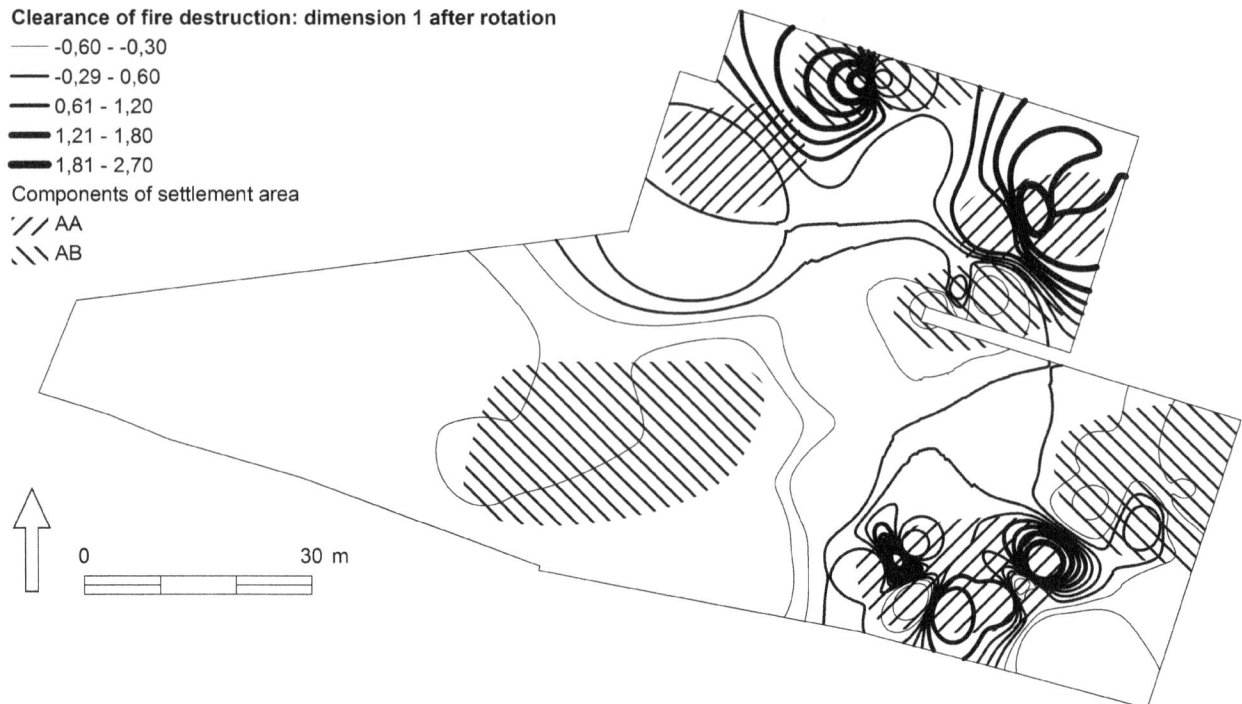

Figure. 8. IDW interpolation of the CATPCA results.

the biplot. The proximity of variables implies positive correlation, while variables on the opposite side of the biplot are negatively correlated.

The biplot reveals a correlation between the proportion of overfired pottery (A), the proportion of large vessels (B) and the fragmentation index (D). It means that overfired pottery more frequently occurred in association with large vessels and with less fragmented pottery. On dimension 1 the group variables have similar loadings as daub density (G) and ceramic density (F) and these are separated from the rest of the variables.

The correlated group of feature attributes (feature area (H), feature depth (I), stratigraphy complexity (J)) shows minor variability in feature morphology: large features are also deeper and have more complicated stratigraphy. The feature attribute group is not correlated (either negatively or positively) to the group of A, B, and D variables. It means that this variable complex is distributed independently of feature morphology and size. Ceramic density is negatively correlated to the feature attribute group. It means that high ceramic density occurs rather in smaller features with a simple stratigraphy.

Heavily abraded pottery (E) is, unsurprisingly, negatively correlated to the fragmentation index. It means that group of A, B, and D variables is associated with the low proportion of heavily abraded pottery.

The proportion of vessel bases (C) does not account for much of the variance on both dimensions.

The results of the CATPCA analysis were subsequently used for spatial analysis. The association of variables A, B, and D was of primary interest. For this reason the two dimensions of the CATPCA analysis were rotated to maximize the component loadings of the variables on dimension 1. Dimension 1 was then used as a variable for IDW interpolation (*figure 8*). Because of the spatial correlation of overfired pottery with the remains of buildings (AA areas), the variable was named "clearance of fire destruction". It is interpreted as the more or less intentional filling of open pits with destructions caused by fire. The less fragmented pottery and the low proportion of heavily abraded pottery were caused by the short depositional history of the pottery.

It is interesting to observe the higher proportion of large vessels in these areas. One explanation is the abovementioned susceptibility of overfired sherds to abrasion, causing a lower probability for thinner sherds of smaller vessels to survive. An alternative explanation is based on the difference between the processes defining a composition of common debris on the one hand, and the remains of fire destruction on the other hand. The proportion of different types of vessels in the area of clearance of fire destruction theoretically reflects more accurately the real vessel proportion in a household. The proportion of large vessels in common pottery debris is probably lower than the proportion in a household due to different vessel uselives. Despite of a variety of ethnoarchaeological data (e.g. DAVID 1972; DAVID – HENNIG 1972; DEBOER 1974; DEBOER 1984; DEBOER – LANTHARP 1979; FOSTER 1960; LONGACRE 1981,

63-64; MAYOR 1994; NELSON 1991; SHOTT 1989) it seems to be a universal trend that vessel uselife increases with vessel size. Large vessels are less frequently discarded and thereby their proportion in the debris is lower. On the other hand the large vessel proportion in material remains of the fire destruction is not biased by vessel uselives. Vessels are broken randomly during a fire according to their position within a structure and actual destruction pattern.

The highest and more even object scores can be observed in the northern part of the analyzed area. The settlement in the area was destroyed by fire, remains of destruction were cleaned up and the area was no longer intensively occupied. A different situation is found in area AA3. There the interpolated surface is irregular and shows a more complicated history of the area. This observation is supported by the chronological analysis. The occupation of the whole analyzed area started in the Bronze Age D – Hallstatt A1 period. In the northern part the occupation ends in the Hallstatt A2 period at the latest while in the southern part it continues to at least Hallstatt B1.

Discussion

The results of the spatial analysis show a spatial correlation between clusters of postholes and the distribution of overfired pottery at the site. The significant presence of overfired pottery in the assemblage is therefore caused by settlement fires rather than pottery technology. If we consider the overfired pottery as a result of settlement fires, we should explain why the Late Bronze Age settlement fires were different from the fires in other periods. The reason could have been a different choice of construction materials (preference of wood and especially straw), perhaps in combination with other factors such as a more open and drier environment of settlement areas.

Wood shortage in deforested landscapes can affect construction traditions. The development in northern Europe of three-aisled houses with two rows of inner posts bearing the roof could be evidence for the adaptation of construction techniques to the changing environment (HARDING 2000, 47; TESCH 1991; 1992, 290). The sophisticated roof construction allows for better redistribution of the stress, thus wood of lower quality and smaller diameters can be used. The overall surface area of the wood in the construction increases, which is crucial for the development and dynamics of burning. Experiments proved that burning of this type of construction could reach temperatures sufficient to overfire ceramics (CHRISTENSEN ET AL. 2007).

But there are not only the material conditions that could change the archeological evidence. Fires are usually viewed in archaeological interpretations as accidental and unintentional events, or as the results of violent behavior. Only in cases where the archaeological evidence is more extensive and regular, an alternative interpretation is given – the intentional destruction of houses by fire as a cultural practice (e.g. KENT 1984, 139–141; NIELSEN 2007, 17; STEVANOVIĆ 1997). There is ethnographic evidence for such practices, usually in the context of site abandonment (e.g. BROOKS 1993, 180–182; MONTGOMERY 1993; SCHLANGER – WILSHUSEN 1993). The reasons for the destruction are mostly ritual: a component of transition rituals between life and death (e.g. DEAL 1985, 269; REICHARD 1990, 81) or magical defense (e.g. JETT – SPENCER 1982, 28; ROTHSCHILD ET AL. 1993, 131).

The intentional destruction of houses by fire seems to be a plausible explanation of the phenomenon of overfired pottery in the Late Bronze Age context considering the archeological evidence, but further analysis needs to be done to test this hypothesis.

Conclusions

Spatial analysis using GIS proved to be a useful analytical tool for testing archaeological hypotheses concerning the origin of overfired pottery in Late Bronze Age settlement. Its application has not created entirely new insights into the phenomenon of overfired pottery, but it founded the interpretation on statistical arguments, which is crucial for creating a constructive discussion. A spatial analysis of course does not put an end to the hypothetical character of archaeological knowledge. The nature of archaeological data is a principal constraint for the interpretation of spatial analysis results. The archaeological record is the result of hardly predictable human actions, much reduced and mixed up by natural processes. There are so many factors involved that there always will be more and less obvious preconditions (explicit in the best case, latent in the worse) structuring and filtering these factors and framing the analysis. Interpretation is then as strong as our knowledge of these preconditions (apart from other methodological aspects of interpretation) and will remain more or less successful as long as it is not falsified.

References Cited:

ARNOLD, D. E. 1978. Ethnography of pottery-making in the valley of Guatemala. In R.K. Wetherington (ed.), *The Ceramics of Kaminaljuyu, Guatemala*, 327-400. University Park, Penn State University Press.

ARNOLD III, P. J. 1991. *Domestic ceramic production and satial oganization: a Mexican case study in ethnoarchaeology*. Cambridge, Cambridge University Press.

BLÁHOVÁ-SKLENÁŘOVÁ, Z. – PROSTŘEDNÍK, J. 2007a. Chronologie sídliště lužických popelnicových polí v Turnově-Maškových zahrádkách. In M. Salaš – K. Šabatová (eds.), *Doba popelnicových polí a doba halštatská. Příspěvky z IX. konference, Bučovice 3. – 6. 10. 2006*, 53–65. Brno, Masarykova univerzita.

BLÁHOVÁ-SKLENÁŘOVÁ, Z. – PROSTŘEDNÍK, J. 2007b. Stavby kultury s lineární keramikou v Turnově-Maškových zahradách. In R. Tichý (ed.), *Otázky neolitu a eneolitu našich zemí: sborník referátů z 25. zasedání badatelů pro výzkum neolitu Čech, Moravy a Slovenska, Kradec Králové 30.10. - 2.11.2006*. Archeologické studie Univerzity Hradec Králové 1, 14–24. Hradec Králové, Gaudeamus.

BROOKS, R. L. 1993. Household abandonment among sedentary Plain societies: behavioral sequence and consequences in the interpretation of the archaeological record. In C.M. Cameron – A.S. Tomka (eds.), *Abandonment of settlements and regions: ethnoarchaeological and archaeological approaches*, 178–191. Cambridge, Cambridge University Press.

CHRISTENSEN, L. B. – JENSEN, S. E. – LUND JOHANSEN, A. L. – JOHANSEN, P. R. – S. LERAGER 2007. House 1 – experimental fire and archaeological excavation. In M. Rasmussen (ed.), *Iron Age houses in flames: Testing house reconstructions at Lejre*. Studies in Technology and Culture 3, 42–133. Lejre, Historical-Archaeological Experimental Centre.

DAVID, N. 1972. On the life span of pottery, type frequencies, and archaeological inference, *American Antiquity* 37(1), 141–142.

DAVID, N. – HENNIG, H. 1972. *The ethnography of pottery: a Fulani case seen in archaeological perspective*. McCaleb module in anthropology, module 21. Reading, Addison-Wesley Pub. Co.

DEAL, M. 1985. Household pottery disposal in the Maya highlands: an ethnoarchaeological interpretation, *Journal of Anthropological Archaeology* 4(4), 243–291.

DEBOER, W. R. 1974. Ceramic longevity and archaeological interpretation: an example from the Upper Ucayali, Peru, *American Antiquity* 39, 335–343.

DEBOER, W. R. 1984. The last pottery show: system and sense in ceramic studies. In S.E. van der Leeuw and A.C. Pritchard (eds.), *The many dimensions of pottery: ceramics in archaeology and anthropology*. CINGULA 7, 529–568. Amsterdam, Institute for Pre- and Protohistory, University of Amsterdam.

DEBOER, W. R. – LANTHARP, D. W. 1979. The making and breaking of Shipibo-Conibo ceramics. In C. Kramer (ed.), *Ethnoarchaeology: implications of ethnography for archaeology*, 102–138. New York, Columbia University Press.

DROBERJAR, E. – PROSTŘEDNÍK, J. 2004. Turnov-Maškovy zahrady - germánský dvorec ze 3. století, *Památky archeologické* 95, 31–106.

FOSTER, G. M. 1960. Life expectancy of utilitarian pottery in Tzintzuntzan, Michoacan, Mexico, *American Antiquity* 25(4), 606–609.

HARDING, A. F. 2000. *European societies in the Bronze Age*. Cambridge, Cambridge University Press.

JETT, S. C. – SPENCER, V. E. 1982. *Navajo architecture: Forms, history, distributions*. Tucson, University of Arizona Press.

KENT, S. 1984. *Analyzing activity areas: an ethnoarchaeological study of the use of space*. Albuquerque, University of New Mexico Press.

KUNA, M. – PROFANTOVÁ, N. (eds.) 2005. *Počátky raného středověku v Čechách. Archeologický výzkum sídelní aglomerace kultury pražského typu v Roztokách*. Praha, Archeologický ústav AV ČR.

LONGACRE, W. A. 1981. Kalinga pottery: an ethnoarchaeological study. In I. Hodder – G. Isaac – N. Hammond (eds.), *Pattern of the past: studies in honour of David Clarke*, 49–66. Cambridge, Cambridge University Press.

MAYOR, A. 1994. Durée de vie des céramiques africaines: facteurs responsables et implications archéologiques. In D. Binder – J. Courtin (eds.), *Terre cuite et société : la céramique, document technique, économique, culturel*. Rencontres Internationales d'Archéologie et d'Historie d'Antibes 14, 179–198. Juan-les-Pins, Editions A.P.D.C.A.

McCOY, J. – JOHNSTON, K. – KOPP, S. – BORUP, B. – WILLISON, J. – PAYNE, B. 2002. *ArcGIS 9: using ArcGIS Spatial Analyst*. Redlands, ESRI.

MEULMAN, J. J. – VAN DER KOOIJ, A. J. – HEISER, W. J. 2004. Principal component analysis with nonlinear optimal scaling trasformations for ordinal and nominal data. In D. Kaplan (ed.), *The Sage handbook of Quantitative methodology for the social sciences*, 49–70. Thousand Oaks - London - New Delhi, Sage Publications.

MONTGOMERY, B. K. 1993. Ceramic analysis as a tool for discovering processes of pueblo abandonment. In C.M. Cameron and A.S. Tomka (eds.), *Abandonment of settlements and regions: ethnoarchaeological and archaeological approaches*, 157–164. Cambridge, Cambridge University Press.

NELSON, B. A. 1991. Ceramic frequency and use-life: a highland Maya case in cross-cultural perspective. In W.A. Longacre (ed.), *Ceramic ethnoarchaeology*, 162–181. Tucson, University of Arizona Press.

NIELSEN, J. N. 2007. The burnt remains of a house from the Pre-Roman Iron Age. In M. Rasmussen (ed.), *Iron Age houses in flames: Testing house reconstructions at Lejre*.

Studies in Technology and Culture 3, 16-31. Lejre, Historical-Archaeological Experimental Centre.

PROSTŘEDNÍK, J. 1999. Výsledky archeologického výzkumu v areálu Maškových zahrad v Turnově aneb existoval zde v mladší době bronzové důležitý komunikační uzel?, *Od Ještěda k Troskám. Vlastivědný sborník Českého ráje a Podještědí* 22(6), 14–18.

PROSTŘEDNÍK, J. 2001. Nové výzkumy sídlišť lidu popelnicových polí na Turnovsku. In V. Vokolek (ed.), *Příspěvky z V. kolokvia „Období popelnicových polí a doba halštatská"*, 97–132. Pardubice, Východočeské muzeum Pardubice.

PROSTŘEDNÍK, J. 2002. Výsledky výzkumu v Turnově-Maškových zahradách v roce 2001, *Zpravodaj muzea v Hradci Králové* 28, 49–53.

REICHARD, G. A. 1990. *Navaho religion: a study of symbolism*. New York, Bollingen Foundation.

ROTHSCHILD, N. A – MILLS, B. J. – FERGUSON, T. J. – DUBLIN, S. 1993. Abandonment at Zuni farming villages. In C.M. Cameron – A.S. Tomka (eds.), *Abandonment of settlements and regions: ethnoarchaeological and archaeological approaches*, 123–137. Cambridge, Cambridge University Press.

SHOTT, M. J. 1989. On tool-class use lives and the formation of archaeological assemblages, *American Antiquity* 54, 9–30.

SCHIFFER, M. B. 1996. *Formation processes of the archaeological record*. Salt Lake City, University of Utah Press.

SCHLANGER, S. H. and WILSHUSEN, R. H. 1993. Local abandonments and regional conditions in the North American Southwest. In C.M. Cameron and A.S. Tomka (eds.), *Abandonment of settlements and regions: ethnoarchaeological and archaeological approaches*, 85–98. Cambridge, Cambridge University Press.

SKLENÁŘOVÁ, Z. 2005. *Obytné stavby doby bronzové – otázky stavebního a konstrukčního vývoje*. Unpublished PhD thesis, Karlova Univerzita.

STEVANOVIĆ, M. 1997. The Age of Clay: The social dynamics of house destruction, *Journal of Anthropological Archaeology* 16, 334–395.

TESCH, S. 1991. Tradition and change during the Bronze Age and Iron Age. Houses as archaeological sources for the study of changes in the cultural landscape In B.E. Berglund (ed.), *The cultural landscape during 6000 years in southern Sweden*. Ecological Bulletins 41, 326–336. Copenhagen, Munksgaard International Booksellers and Publishers.

TESCH, S. 1992. House, farm and village in the Köpinge area from Early Neolithic to Early Middle Ages In L. Larsson – J. Callmer – B. Stjernquist (eds.), *The archaeology of the cultural landscape: field work and research in a south Swedish rural region*. Acta Archaeologica Ludensia 19, 283–344. Stockholm, Almqvist and Wiksell.

THÉR, R. 2009. *Technologie výpalu keramiky a její vztah k organizaci a specializaci ve výrobě keramiky v kontextu kultur popelnicových polí*. Unpublished PhD thesis, Masarykova univerzita.

TSCHOPIK, H. 1950. An Andean ceramic tradition in historical perspective, *American Antiquity* 15(3), 196–218.

WAANE, S. 1977. Pottery Making Traditions of the Ikombe Kisi, Mbeya Region, Tanzania, *Baessler-Archiv* 25(2), 251–306.

Richard Thér
Department of Archaeology, Faculty of Arts,
University of Hradec Králové
Rokitanského 62
500 03 Hradec Kralové
richard.ther@uhk.cz

Jan Prostředník
The Museum of the Bohemian Paradise
Skálova 71
511 01 Turnov
prostrednik@muzeum-turnov.cz